A really good biography does more than tell a story: it inspires and it imparts wisdom. That is precisely what this book does. Eryl Davies not only shines a light on an undervalued hero of the faith; he lets the reader taste Thomas Charles' own love for Christ and the Scriptures. May the Lord use this to raise up more like him.

Mike Reeves
President and Professor of Theology, Union School of Theology, Wales

This is a brilliantly written little book about a person who deserves to be better known than he is today, for his ministry and influence extended to all parts of Britain and the island of Ireland, not to mention other countries of the world. It is written from the perspective of God's providential dealings with this man of God who saw even insignificant events as under God's control and for His good purposes. The book will inform, challenge and encourage twenty-first century Christians and churches worldwide. Buy it, read it and see for yourself!

Philip Eveson
Former Principal, London Theological Seminary
Minister, Kensit Evangelical Church, Finchley, London

The Puritan John Flavel wrote: 'The Providence of God is like Hebrew words – it can be read only backwards.' In this heart-warming book on the life of Thomas Charles, Eryl Davies helps us get a glimpse into the providence of God that changed not only one life, but the lives of many, many others around the world. Exploring his conversion, lessons learnt at university, a romantic pursuit that lasted nearly a decade, opposition, struggles, loss, illness, and revival, this is a book that will encourage and challenge.

Jonathan Thomas
Pastor, Cornerstone Church, Abergavenny
Author and BBC Radio Wales presenter and contributor

The ripples of Charles' ministry and influence – not least in his involvement in establishing the British and Foreign Bible Society – have touched many lands beyond the regions of the UK and Ireland. May this highly readable biography encourage us to pray for the birth and growth of the Church amongst indigenous groups across the world today who are discovering that God speaks into their lives in the language of their heart too. And may the younger generations of peoples who once knew the reality of the awesome, life-and-society-transforming presence and power of the Spirit of the living Christ among them, discover that He is the same yesterday, today and forever and well worth trekking across mountains to encounter – even if, in our softness, we may well wear a pair of robust, waterproof boots in our quest!

Hector Morrison
Principal of Highland Theological College, Dingwall, Scotland

A hearty welcome to Dr Davies' charming, searching, and inspiring primer on the life and times of Thomas Charles. To many, Charles is unknown, vaguely known, or a statue in the tourist town of Bala, North Wales. Here, though, is a timely opportunity to be enriched by his God-empowered, gospel-shaped, Word-mediated impact on the darkness of his day. Learn amid the present confusion of Charles' healthy balancing of the Word and the Spirit. In waiting on God for days of refreshing, be energised by Charles' industry and entrepreneurialism in the cause of the gospel. Dr. Davies' compelling narrative not only aids the recovery of Thomas Charles, it strengthens hope that we might see a like movement of God's grace and power.

Tim J. R. Trumper
President, His Fullness Ministries

No Difficulties with God is a compelling, well written and well researched book by Dr D. Eryl Davies. In it we encounter not only the life and works of Thomas Charles, but also so much of Dr Davies' passion for this gigantic figure. He gives us a fresh insight into the life and Christian witness of a man not only known nationally in Wales but also further afield in Ireland, Scotland and internationally through his alliance with organizations such as the London Missionary Society.

Throughout the book, there is a commanding plea for us today to acquaint ourselves with a new appreciation of what made Thomas Charles a person 'who found no difficulties with God'. Read and be enthralled.

W. Bryn Williams
Minister, Pwllheli Presbyterian Pastorate
Academic Director, Presbyterian Church of Wales
/Gweinidog Gofalaeth Pwllhel & Cyfarwyddwr Academaidd EBC

No Difficulties with God

with God

The Life of Thomas Charles, Bala

(1755-1814)

D. Eryl Davies

CHRISTIAN
FOCUS

Hardback ISBN 978-1-5271-0847-9
Ebook ISBN 978-1-5271-0923-0

A CIP catalogue record for this book is available from the British Library.

10 9 8 7 6 5 4 3 2 1

Published in 2022
by
Christian Focus Publications Ltd,
Geanies House, Fearn, Ross-shire,
IV20 1TW, Scotland, Great Britain

www.christianfocus.com

Designed by Daniel Van Straaten

Printed by Gutenberg, Malta

Contents

Llanycil Church building. Now the Mary Jones Centre, on the edge of Bala town.

The gravestone of Thomas Charles, his wife, and child, in the cemetery in front of Llanycil Parish church situated on the edge of Bala and alongside Bala lake.

The house where Thomas Charles lived and where his wife and her parents had a shop. Located in the main High Street in Bala.

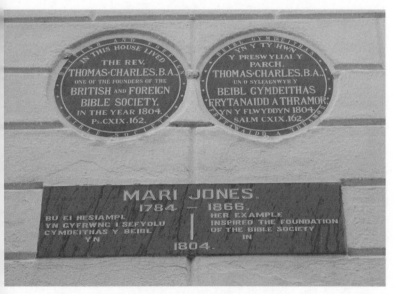

The plaque on the wall of the house above. Text (above) reads: 'The Rev. Thomas Charles, B.A., one of the founders of the British and Foreign Bible Society, in the year 1804.' Text (below): 'Mary Jones. 1784–1866. Her example inspired the foundation of the Bible Society in 1804.'

Bala lake from the shore line of Bala town.

The Thomas Charles column is in the heart of the town and only yards away from where he once lived. The column is outside the Welsh Presbyterian church with which Charles had close links in its early history.

Preface

———————————————————

Thomas Charles was a household name in Wales at least until the mid-twentieth century. The moving story of the young teenager Mary Jones walking about twenty-six miles alone over the mountains to Bala to buy her personal copy of the Bible from Thomas Charles remains popular especially amongst children and young people, serving to draw attention to Charles' work in obtaining copies of the Bible for people in Wales and other countries. Charles was famous as a preacher, theologian, scholar and educationalist; he was not only renowned for securing adequate supplies of Welsh Bibles but also for supporting the translation and distribution of the Bible in different languages for overseas mission. In many respects, he was a giant of a man greatly admired in Wales and England as well as in Ireland and Scotland. Without Charles' gifted leadership and his unstinting labours, Calvinistic Methodism[1] in Wales, which developed rapidly during his lifetime in tandem with local and regional revivals, would

---

1 In 1933 the Calvinistic Methodist or Presbyterian Church of Wales Act in Parliament granted equal standing to both names. As the last century progressed the Calvinistic Methodists increasingly used the new name, Presbyterian Church of Wales *(Eglwys Bresbyteraidd Cymru)*.

have degenerated into emotionalism and unbiblical teaching. The Bible was of first importance for Charles as was also knowing and enjoying the Lord revealed in the Word. For Charles, doctrine, faith and love for the Lord must always be expressed in consistent holy living and a passion for the gospel.

I am persuaded that Thomas Charles needs to be rediscovered by new generations of Christians and listened to seriously in the twenty-first century for we can profit much from his life and labours. I have found it challenging and refreshing to read again his many letters and recall all that he did out of love for his Saviour, the Lord Jesus Christ. It has been an enormous privilege to write this biography from the perspective of divine providence which was hugely important for Charles though it has not been given the attention it merits by historians.

In writing this book, I have used the massive but invaluable three-volume biography by D.E. Jenkins[2] of Charles' life which has been a joy to re-read, despite the excessive detail provided. Jenkins' biography includes many original letters written by Charles and others. Charles' other writings have been revisited as have some secondary sources.[3]

One word of explanation before proceeding. I have taken the liberty of referring to the subject of this biography as 'Charles' and this is deliberate for that is how Sally often addressed him in her letters to him. I am following her example!

---

2 D.E. Jenkins, *The Rev. Thomas Charles BA of Bala,* (Denbigh: Llewelyn Jenkins, 1910) volumes 1, 2 & 3; abbreviated to DEJ in all other references to this work with Roman numerals indicating the volume.

3 I am also grateful to Dr John Aaron for allowing me to read an early draft of his extensive biography of *Thomas Charles of Bala (1755–1814)* which represents the most thorough research on his life and work. This work has been published by Banner of Truth Trust (2022).

My prayer in commending this book to you is that the Lord will use it to stir Christians in understanding and benefitting more from the Lord's provision of His Word and the precious Holy Spirit. That is the only way of knowing, honouring and enjoying our union with Christ in more intimate ways. Theologically, the believer's *union* with Christ is secure but our *communion* or fellowship with Christ sadly is variable and may leave a lot to be desired. Charles calls us to *commune intimately* with our risen, exalted Lord but then also to proclaim Him passionately to the whole world. This is our privilege and responsibility as Christians in the twenty-first century, but above all else may our triune God, Father, Son and Holy Spirit increasingly receive all the glory for ever and ever.

Eryl Davies
Cardiff,
Summer 2021

Foreword

<hr/>

Any historical retelling of the eighteenth-century Welsh Methodist revival must touch upon certain iconic events and persons. For instance, how could we begin to recount the events of the Protestant Reformation without stalwarts like Martin Luther and John Calvin or the Great Awakening without the towering figures of Jonathan Edwards and George Whitefield? Similarly, central to the outpouring of God's Spirit in Wales and beyond are men like Daniel Rowland, William Williams, and Howell Harris. Repeatedly absent from this storyline is the often-overlooked preacher of Bala, Thomas Charles. Though not yet born when Howell Harris was converted at a church in his hometown of Talgarth in 1735, which is regularly regarded as the immediate beginnings of the revival, Thomas Charles is sometimes deemed a second-generation figure within Welsh Calvinist Methodism. However, though a bit later chronologically, Charles' contribution to Welsh revivalism, education, biblicism, and spirituality is no less significant than his forefathers in the faith.

It is a tremendous privilege to recommend to a new generation of readers this spiritually robust volume of the life of Thomas Charles.

My friend, Eryl Davies, weaves together a portrait of a man with a driving passion for the Lord Jesus Christ – knowing Him, loving Him, and proclaiming Him. Unlike the dusty biographical accounts detached from experience, the readers of this remarkable life will themselves enjoy basking in the eternal rays of the glory of God in the face of Jesus Christ that shone so refulgently in the life and ministry of Thomas Charles. Never glossing over his flaws as a sinner saved by grace, Davies sets Charles forward as a great spiritual model for his readers and a gift to the whole of evangelicalism in Wales and throughout the Christian world. From his arduous efforts of Christian instruction through his prolific preaching ministry, Sunday schools, teaching catechisms, establishing circulating schools, production and editing of Bibles, and writing other literary works, Charles demonstrated that the fruit of revival is not only an awakening of the heart but also a renewal of the mind.

If allowed to speak, I believe Thomas Charles would desire us to look beyond the mere story of God's providence in the life of man to the ravishing joy of dwelling eternally in the presence of our sovereign God. It's with this perspective in view that we live a life wholly dedicated, not to ourselves, but to the propagation of the gospel of Jesus Christ and to the glory of our heavenly Father with whom 'there are no difficulties.'

Dustin Benge
Associate Professor of biblical spirituality/historical theology and
Vice President of Communications
The Southern Baptist Theological Seminary, Louisville, Kentucky

1 Exciting But Challenging

You may know little about Thomas Charles (1755–1814) and may need a reminder of what you read or heard about him years ago. Or perhaps you have never heard of him. If so, here is a biography relating the story of how God prepared, saved and used this man in remarkable ways. It is the story of someone who knew God deeply and lived in a revival period. He was a giant in the faith and recognised as a key Christian leader within Wales and far beyond.

Suspense

There are elements of suspense in the story. Perplexing situations, unexpected twists and turns, then a romance in which he woos the young lady he loves for years. There was regular, sometimes fierce, opposition to the gospel he preached before the story breaks out into successful, though demanding, church planting involving considerable travel, not to mention exhaustion, even frostbite. He wrote resources for young and old, so they could understand the Christian faith and also developed circulating schools and Sunday schools throughout Wales. Burdened to distribute Welsh Bibles, he

19

then helped establish the British and Foreign Bible Society, serving as a director in missionary and charitable societies in London. He knew and cooperated with key evangelical clergy and laypeople in England who also supported his work. Charles also encouraged and advised Christians both in Ireland and Scotland in developing schools, advocating Bible translation in Irish and Gaelic and the distribution of the Scriptures. In Wales, Charles witnessed the gospel preached in extraordinary power on occasions. The Lord was saving many people while believers rejoiced in Christ. There is much more to tell so please read on.

Young

The Lord has often used young people in strategic, critical periods in the history of the Christian Church. Luther, Calvin, Zwingli and others in the sixteenth-century Protestant Reformation in Europe were all young when converted, then thrust into the forefront of the Lord's work to preach God's Word with its message of saving grace in Christ. Their task was humanly impossible in facing the spiritual darkness of Europe, the fierce opposition of kings and the stranglehold of Roman Catholicism. But the Lord used these young men to bring back the gospel to Europe.

This happened too in Wales early in the eighteenth-century with the immediate predecessors of Thomas Charles when young men were saved and called to ministries in revival which profoundly influenced Wales. Daniel Rowland (1713–1790) was a young curate in Llangeitho, West Wales, when converted at the age of twenty-two and Howell Harris (1714–1773) came to Christ and assurance of forgiveness when only twenty-one. William Williams (1717–1791) became a Christian aged twenty-one in 1738. Immediately they were thrown into the forefront of the Lord's work.

Similarly, Thomas Charles became a Christian while a teenager and later led the Calvinistic Methodists in Wales, filling the gap following the deaths of first-generation leaders. Charles became 'one of the greatest figures in the history of Wales',[1] whose contribution to the Christian church was incalculable and long-lasting.

It is a privilege to introduce you to Thomas Charles. Be careful, however – the story is challenging and searching in unexpected ways.

---

1 Gwyn Davies *A Light in the Land: Christianity in Wales 200-2000,* (Bridgend: Bryntirion Press, 2002), p. 84.

2 Becoming a Christian

Aged ten, Charles met an elderly Christian man who became a great help to him in explaining and commending the Christian faith. He was Rees Hugh. Although living 'a few miles' away, Charles visited him at least weekly to hear him talk lovingly and warmly about Jesus Christ. Charles was encouraged listening to him, regarding him as 'my father in Christ' and loved the aged saint dearly. More about this later.

Providence

Providence was a key doctrine for Charles – the Creator-God sustains but also rules over the entire world, including people everywhere and all events, big or small. He works out His wise and good purpose in all that happens so we are not controlled by impersonal fate or chance but by a personal, living God. Even insignificant details and events are all under God's complete control and within His good purpose. In his famous and influential *Geiriadur Ysgrythurol* (Bible Dictionary) Charles describes providence in some depth.[1] He reminds readers that different words are used in the Bible to describe God's

1 Parch Thomas Charles, B.A, *Geiriadur Ysgrythur* (Scriptural Dictionary), (Bala: R. Saunderson, 1864, 6th Impression), pp. 770-1.

providential purpose as in Acts 4:28, Romans 8:28-30, 1 Corinthians 2:7 and Ephesians 1:5, 9-11. God does not do anything without a wise, righteous but good purpose, though often His actions are beyond our understanding. God's absolute control and plan in all things worldwide has a special application in fulfilling the divine plan of salvation for the elect through Jesus Christ. In that light Charles could say: 'At last providence brought me acquainted with an aged, holy, and pious man, by name, Rees Hugh…' For Charles, providence was vitally important for understanding life and the world as well as his personal circumstances and the work given him to do. In the twenty-first century Christians ought to give more attention to this teaching and trust God whatever the circumstances may be.

Providence illustrated

Thomas Charles was born in 1755 near St Clears in Carmarthenshire, South West Wales. His family rented a large farm but his father, a respected church warden, was not a successful farmer which led to financial difficulties. The young child had several siblings and his mother exercised considerable influence on his early years. In God's providence, the area where Charles lived had a Christian background dating back to the mid-sixteenth century but it was a local vicar, Griffith Jones (1684–1761) in Llanddowror, who influenced Charles but only indirectly for he died five years before Charles attended the parish school there.

Griffith Jones preached extensively in Wales and many people were converted through him. One strategic aspect of Jones's work was establishing schools in the country. His schools were different from those of today for they circulated around Wales, remaining in one locality for three months. As very few people were able to read, the purpose of these schools was to teach children in the daytime to read and then adults in the evenings. Jones thought three months was adequate time for all to learn to read. Jones was also involved in appointing and training the teachers and collecting money from wealthy people and charities to support the schools. Those attending the schools were taught to read the Welsh Bible and taught the Catechism of the Church of England.[2] The population in Wales at this time was just over half a million people but nearly half the population had been taught to read through these schools, becoming acquainted with the Bible and its message. Thomas Charles was able to build upon and extend considerably this massive contribution.

When probably eleven years of age, Charles was sent to the parish church school in Llanddowror where he studied for three years until he was fourteen years of age. Here he would hear more about Griffith Jones and develop a more serious interest in the Christian faith, becoming more aware of sin in his life and regularly walking several miles to hear the gospel preached. Christian books also helped him and he felt the need to share with others his thoughts about the Christian faith. In that respect he felt lonely so valued meeting Rees Hugh, walking several miles, sometimes twice a week, to see him. Rees Hugh had come to trust the Lord through Griffith Jones's ministry, for Charles describes him as 'an old disciple of Mr Griffith Jones of Llanddowror'. Clearly 'his conversation', writes Thomas Charles, 'was much blessed to me'. How was he helped by Rees Hugh? Several clues are provided in what he wrote later in life. One fact was the 'great joy' the man had when sharing about the Lord Jesus. Being a Christian was not a miserable, boring affair for him. Far from it. He loved and knew Christ so well that he delighted

---

2 The *Catechism of the Church of England* (1662); Jones wrote his own *Catechism* in 1752 which expanded the former.

in talking about the Lord. Charles explains he 'never was unaffected' by listening to Rees Hugh and remembered him with great affection. Rees Hugh also prayed for the young Charles.

Despite this friendship, Thomas Charles was not a Christian. He sought answers to questions about the Christian faith and decided to receive Holy Communion in the parish church. He wanted to become a Christian and throughout this period he was also helped by the kindness, understanding and love of his family.

Afraid

At the age of fourteen, Thomas Charles suddenly became afraid. There was a feeling of 'dread' on his part. Referring to Rees Hugh, Charles adds: 'My old dear friend was very fearful and anxious for me in my new situation.' The 'new situation' was his father's decision to send him to Carmarthen Academy for further studies. The Academy had a long and varied history in terms of location and belief with its nominal, religious influence despite the different theological views of tutors. Academic standards were high, possibly the best in Wales, so Charles, despite his 'dread', would receive an excellent education there. His friend, Rees Hugh, 'prayed earnestly with me and for me before I went', writes Charles, 'and I have often thought I have received many blessings in answer to his prayers to God for me.' Although he did not realise at the time, in providence God was preparing Charles for his future work by directing him to the Academy. For example, one tutor gave Thomas Charles a great love for Latin, Greek and Hebrew. Later in his life he wrote: 'I have no greater pleasure in the world … than reading the Holy Scriptures in the languages in which the Holy Spirit delivered them; namely the Old Testament in Hebrew, and the New Testament in Greek.' Charles used the biblical languages well later so here was another example of God's wise providence preparing the teenager for his future work. His father's decision was a wise one.

Conversion

There were temptations facing the teenager in the Academy but a further providence was that he lodged with his older sister Elizabeth and her husband Joseph Thomas, respected merchants in Carmarthen. This was a considerable help for Charles in adapting to a new situation and being confronted by many challenges and snares.

Another aspect of God's providence is that during his studies in Carmarthen, Charles attended the local 'Methodist' society. Methodism was a spontaneous, later an organised, movement within the Church of England for many decades, emphasising a personal and joyful experience of God's grace in Christ. They accepted major Bible doctrines, emphasising God's eternal plan to save a vast number of sinful people; for them Christ died to redeem them from the guilt, power and punishment of sin. Only God by the Holy Spirit could awaken and change sinners inwardly, leading them to personal faith in Christ then protecting and blessing them in union with Christ until they reached heaven. Charles benefitted from hearing those in the society talking about the Lord Jesus and knowing Him personally. However, for the first three years in the Academy, Charles had not become a Christian although he continued to read Christian books.

'Happy day'

The 20 January 1773 was an important date for the seventeen-year-old student. It was 'a day much to be remembered by me as long as I live'. He often referred back in thankfulness to God for what happened on this date. Charles had gone some distance to hear the well-known Daniel Rowland[3] preach; his text was Hebrews 4 verse 15: 'For we do not have a High Priest who cannot sympathise with our weaknesses, but was in all points tempted as we are, yet without sin' (NKJV).

What happened? Charles explains: 'I had such a view of Christ as our High Priest, of his love, compassion, power, and all-sufficiency, as filled my soul with astonishment – with joy unspeakable and full of glory.' Charles was convicted of his sin and unbelief, including the hard views of God he had retained. Now in seeing the Lord's amazing love and unlimited power, his mind 'was overwhelmed and overpowered with amazement'.[4] It was so amazing what he heard that he felt it was too good to be true! 'I could not believe for very joy,' he explains. Five years later he refers back to this date: '…a special day, to be greatly remembered. So glorious was the revelation of divine truths… By mercy they are … as glorious and valuable as ever, they are always new, always awakening.' Although he believed gospel truths before and enjoyed talking with Christians about the Lord, Charles now experienced the power and reality of the gospel in a deeply personal way. He confessed: 'I had some idea of gospel truths before floating in my head, but they never powerfully and with divine energy penetrated my heart until now.' He had now become a Christian. Eight years later he insisted that on the 20 January 1773, 'the light of the knowledge of the glorious gospel first shone brightly in my soul in the face of Jesus Christ.'

Whether a person can date conversion so precisely as Charles is unimportant, for many come to saving faith in Christ over a period of

---

3 Daniel Rowland (1711–90) was a curate in the parish church of Llangeitho in rural West Wales. He ministered here powerfully for fifty years, and attracted large congregations from all over Wales.

4 DEJ, 1, 31.

time. Charles himself had been on a journey over several years when suddenly the Lord dealt with him under the preaching of the gospel. What is essential is personal faith in Jesus Christ as Saviour and Lord resulting from a supernatural, inward work of the Holy Spirit giving new life and a radically new nature to love, trust and obey the Lord.

For two more years Thomas Charles studied in Carmarthen Academy and though tempted often 'God's invisible hand preserved me – the everlasting arms were underneath.' He also enjoyed rich fellowship with other Christians, the powerful preaching of the gospel 'and also much of the divine presence in them'.

In the Lord's providence, a huge surprise lay ahead of him.

3 1775 and 1777: Significant Years

A complete surprise and no one in his family anticipated it. Nor had Charles imagined such a change in his circumstances would be possible. And it's that word 'providence' again. God ordered circumstances in this unexpected way to prepare Charles for his future work, but there were big lessons to learn and also relearn.

1775: 'no difficulties with God'

The year was 1775 and, to his amazement, Charles was a student at Jesus College, Oxford. He explains: 'Providence very unexpectedly and very wonderfully opened my way to Oxford.' He affirms his family had not 'the least idea of it till just at this time, but now all obstacles were removed and it was determined I should go.' The way the Lord worked this providence gave the young Charles 'great satisfaction and strong assurance'. He concluded: 'There are no difficulties with God. Difficulties wholly exist in our unbelieving hearts.' Trusting the Lord, he accepted 'cheerfully and submissively' the Lord's providence regarding Oxford.[1]

---

1   DEJ, 1, 38-9.

What made study in Oxford possible? We do not know. It would have been appropriate for him to continue studies in Carmarthen Academy and apply later to become an Anglican curate. Others had taken that route. His academic ability was excellent so that was not a barrier. He matriculated in late May 1775 so met all the requirements of university entrance. Financially too it was feasible for him to have continued as a student in Carmarthen as the costs were reduced due to lodging with his sister and her husband; his parents also visited him regularly providing food and other necessities. The family could not have supported him in Oxford financially so a donor unexpectedly financed his studies there. Was it a legacy from his late grandmother's estate that made the difference? Whatever the source of income, the family decided quickly for him to study in Oxford in that the money was now available.

Encouraged

On the journey to Oxford, Charles was assured the Lord had opened the way for him to study in Oxford University. The Lord's words greatly encouraged him: 'I am ascending to My Father and your Father, and to My God and your God' (John 20:17). These words, he explained, 'sounded melodiously in my ears'. He explained the comfort he received from those words: 'On the road the Lord gave me very comfortable views of himself as my Father in Christ; that Christ's Father was my Father and his God my God. What could I want more! Here was power sufficient and compassion enough! I was enabled thro' grace to commit myself to the custody of my heavenly Father and to yield myself cheerfully and submissively to the guidance of his Spirit and Providence.' He arrived in Oxford on the 26 May 1775. A further encouragement was that his uncle had studied in the same college and was a vicar only a few miles away so he would be able to visit him for advice.

Friends

Charles was eager to meet new Christian friends in university and the friendships he made and cultivated were a great help while in Oxford as well as in future years. Among his friends, some deserve mention.

One close friend was **John Mayor** (1755–1826) who had a Welsh background and was ordained to the Anglican ministry in 1778 like Charles. Mayor served in the curacies of famous evangelical clergy like William Rose (1751–1829), John Newton (1725–1807) and John Berridge (1716–1793), then became a vicar near Shrewsbury in the parish of Shawbury for forty years. Charles often preached there over the years. Another student friend was **Edward Griffin** (1755–1833), nearly two years ahead of Charles in his studies, but their friendship continued after Oxford when Griffin settled as a vicar in Ipswich following a number of curacies. Griffin's considerable interest in, and support for, the Church Missionary Society may have strengthened Charles' later concern for the wider distribution of the Bible.

Watts Wilkinson (1755–1840) was also a valued Oxford friend. Ordained into the Anglican ministry and given various appointments before lecturing for many years in two London churches on Sunday afternoons and Tuesday mornings, 'his churches were always crowded…'. Wilkinson provides us with an insight into the value of his friendship with Charles while a student in Oxford. Referring to 'the pain of parting' with friends like Charles especially and also Mayor, he testifies: 'How often have I trudged from Worcester (College) to Jesus College with low spirits and a heavy heart, but, cheered with my dear friend's pious and enlivening conversation, have returned cheerful and rejoicing. I protest, my heart sinks within me, while I call to mind the spots we have frequented, the conversations we have held, the prayers we have joined in!' These words indicate the strength of Charles' own faith and the lively manner in which he conversed with others about the Lord. The fellowship these friends enjoyed was rich as they majored on prayer, sharing details of the Lord's personal dealings with them alongside the comforts of Scripture. They also talked about books they were reading. Although separated by many miles after leaving Oxford, these friends remained in contact, diligently praying for each other and sharing details of their work for many years.

One more friend Charles enjoyed fellowship with in Oxford was **Simon Lloyd** (1756–1836) who started studies in Jesus College, Oxford, a few days beforehand. Lloyd was later ordained into the Anglican ministry, serving as a curate outside Bristol then moving in turn to three different parishes in North Wales, the last one being the church in Llanycil, on the outskirts of the market town of Bala. Like Charles, he faced opposition in his parishes because his 'Methodism', a term referring to his clear biblical convictions and gospel preaching, was resented by the people. From 1800 he was without a parish church and began to work closely with Charles in North Wales for years, fruitfully preaching the Word and encouraging converts, particularly within the Calvinist Methodist movement.

All four friends shared Charles' desire to love and serve the Lord Jesus by proclaiming the gospel.

1777: Crisis

After nearly two happy years as a student in Oxford, Charles faced a crisis. It was totally unexpected. Charles felt perplexed and distressed at the possibility now of being unable to continue his studies and graduating. The crisis was a financial one: 'My supplies from Wales were at once stopped.' He was 'exceedingly puzzled' concerning this sudden change in providence. Nevertheless, though there appeared to be no one he could turn to for financial support, rather than panic and despair, Charles' attitude was one of being 'perfectly submissive to the Lord's will'.[2] He was convinced that the Lord in His goodness and wisdom was in charge of his new circumstance. Although admitting he was 'puzzled' as to what was happening in his life yet he had a 'secret trust' that the Lord 'would direct and provide' for him.

'Very thankful'

'One morning as I was writing to my friends in Wales informing them of my difficulties and my consequent resolution' to leave Oxford, he writes, his friend John Mayor called, 'to whom I immediately explained my situation and also the resolution I had formed of leaving Oxford.' It must have been a relief to unburden himself, but Mayor was shocked hearing the news and was extremely unhappy with Charles' decision to leave Oxford. He asked Charles to delay his departure from Oxford for a few days as he felt certain help would become available from somewhere, though unknown to them. The advice was wise and Charles accepted his suggestion. A 'few days after', writes Charles, 'A gentleman in Oxford sent for me to dine with him; I went and before we parted, to my great surprise, he produced the £20 I wanted.' At that time £20 was a considerable amount of money and would have met all his immediate needs. Surprisingly, the man promised that Charles would not be in need financially while he remained a student in Oxford. Was the donor a prominent person and local shopkeeper? We do not know but his promise to care for Charles financially while he was in Oxford was a remarkable answer

2 DEJ, 1, 41-2.

to prayer and encouragement to trust God in similar future situations. Charles 'much rejoiced', being 'very thankful' to the donor and to the Lord. In God's providence, the donor honoured his promise but also introduced Charles to a wider circle of Christians which would have significance for him in the future. Charles never forgot how his friend John Mayor visited and advised him in this crisis. Two years later, for example, he wrote to Mayor to thank him 'for the friendly assistance you *gave*, as well as *procured'*, enabling him to complete his studies in university in God's wise plan while also encouraging him to believe Bible promises concerning God's detailed care and providence. It was a necessary lesson. He was learning and relearning to trust God in all circumstances, whatever the difficulties or disappointments.

Tensions ahead

Charles and his four friends were Anglicans, nurtured in that church with Charles having been profoundly influenced by Anglican clergy in Wales like Griffith Jones and Daniel Rowland. As Oxford University only admitted at this time those who belonged to the state church, it was providential that Charles and his friends were committed to serving the church. While the number of evangelical Anglican clergy in Wales were few and scattered, in England there were many more evangelical curates and vicars, some of whom will be referred to in the next chapter. Charles would soon be introduced to some of these key men and build lasting relationships with them.

Tensions, however, existed between the Anglican Church and the emerging 'Methodism' in both Wales and England, a tension which Charles and Lloyd would be caught up in later. An illustration of this early tension is evident in the ministry of the famous Griffith Jones, rector of Llanddowror in Carmarthenshire. Jones became a well-known preacher in churches and in the open air in which many people were converted, but an even greater influence was exercised through the schools he established throughout the country. In these schools, adults and children were taught to read the Bible, and godly teachers then explained the gospel message resulting in many scholars being converted and established in the Christian faith. To meet the spiritual needs of those saved, 'societies' were established which were informal fellowships majoring on prayer, exhortation from the Bible and the sharing of the Lord's dealings with them. By 1750, approximately 350 societies had been formed in South Wales and 82 in North Wales. These societies came under the umbrella of the 'Methodists', a movement within the Anglican Church which emphasised a vibrant saving relationship to God through the substitutionary sacrifice of Jesus Christ on the cross for sin. Because of the large numbers of people responding to the gospel and attending society meetings, laymen were appointed – called 'exhorters' – to lead the meetings and provide biblical teaching and oversight. The title 'exhorters' was meant to reassure suspicious clergy and bishops that they were not regarded as ordained ministers.

Nevertheless, tensions arose. Even the Rev. Griffith Jones in Wales became unhappy with the growth of Methodism and later reduced his itinerary preaching and disliked the 'excitement' he felt existed amongst converts. Thomas Charles, too, in Oxford was aware of the tension, showing himself faithful to the Anglican Church. Even though he had attended the Methodist Society when in Carmarthen, he felt that one student acted 'indiscreetly' by attending services in Wesleyan Methodist chapels, yet the university had reacted harshly by withholding his degree. At the time, Charles would not personally have attended those chapels, but he soon discovered that rejection of his biblical preaching in parish churches would in God's providence drive him increasingly into the fold of the Calvinistic

Methodist movement in Wales. That cloud lay ahead, but Charles was not yet ready to face the serious implications and cost involved.

In the next chapter we describe the last year of his studies in Oxford and some surprising, new relationships he formed. He was being led in God's wise providence.

4 A Special Visit

•————————————————————————————————————•

Thomas Charles was excited. There was good reason too for him to feel excited. At the end of their second year of studies in Oxford in 1777, he and his friend, John Mayor, received a personal invitation from the well-known Rev. John Newton to spend three months of their summer vacation with Newton in his home and church. To understand their excitement and joy, we need to step back to appreciate the wider church situation.

Gospel preachers

Charles was aware of a growing number of faithful and well-known gospel preachers in parish churches in England. They were influential as there was considerable blessing and growth in their churches. Some of these men would be supportive of Charles in the future.

One man was the learned **John Berridge** (1716–1793) who became a vicar in Everton, Bedfordshire. J.C. Ryle described him as 'a mighty instrument for good' whose preaching was understood by ordinary folk; he travelled on horseback through the counties of Cambridgeshire, Bedfordshire and Hertfordshire, preaching ten or twelve times a week, sometimes outside to thousands of people. His parish church was crowded with people eager to hear him preach.

Another important name is **William Romaine** (1714–1795), evangelical rector at St Anne's, Blackfriars, London. A former Oxford student, he was a competent Hebrew Bible scholar who became a leader amongst London evangelicals. His parish church ministry was very influential. He preached there at least four times a week for years expounding the entire Bible. Charles soon had the privilege of meeting him.

John Newton (1725–1807) was Curate-in-Charge of the parish church, St Peter & St Paul in Olney, Buckinghamshire and lived in the rectory opposite the church. He quickly gained a reputation for excellent preaching, counselling and writing books as well as numerous hymns like *'Amazing grace! how sweet the sound that saved a wretch like me'*, and *'How sweet the name of Jesus sounds in a believer's ear'*. He was in regular touch with fellow evangelical clergymen and was sought after for his wise counselling.

Newton's conversion had been life-changing. He had spent turbulent years with his father, a ship's captain, at sea before being employed on a merchant ship involved in the Africa slave trade. His life became immoral and worldly, but a frightening incident at sea forced him to pray and read the Bible. He dates this incident as 21 March 1748 and several months later he was converted. After more voyages and his marriage in 1755, Newton took the job of Tide Surveyor at the Port of Liverpool while studying the Bible and theology before being ordained into the Church of England ministry in 1764. Newton began a successful ministry in Olney where the church attendance grew so much that it became necessary for a gallery to be built for the growing numbers attending services. In 1769, he began a Thursday prayer service, often writing a hymn to be sung to a familiar tune. He also challenged William Cowper who attended the church to write a hymn regularly for this meeting which he did until he became seriously ill in 1773. In 1780 Newton moved to an important parish, St Mary Woolnoth Church in London where his main work was preaching. Here he contributed even more significantly to the nurturing of spiritual life and biblical understanding within the Anglican Church as well as supporting the work of the Committee for the Abolition of the Slave Trade, formed in 1787. As a result of William Wilberforce (1759–1833) meeting with Newton on numerous occasions over the years and receiving wise advice, Wilberforce decided against entering the ministry of the church but rather remaining a Member of Parliament and he became the voice of the abolitionist movement in Parliament. Newton's death in 1807 occurred only a few months after the Act abolishing the slave trade throughout the British Empire had been approved. It was with this influential clergyman Charles and Mayor spent the summer of 1777.

There were other evangelical clergy in the Church of England but due to their influence I refer only to three of them. **Thomas Haweis** (1734–1820) studied in Oxford before being ordained in 1757. He became the rector of Aldwincle, Northamptonshire, until his retirement in 1809. His church exercised a significant influence in the area while Haweis himself became a co-founder of the London Missionary Society.

Richard Cecil (1748–1810), a former Oxford student, served in three parish churches – Thornton, Bagworth and Markfield – in Leicestershire before becoming rector at Lewes, eventually settling at St John's Chapel, Bedford Row, London where he ministered for eighteen years. Here he often preached as many as four sermons a day. Mention too must be made of **Charles Simeon** (1759–1836), a Cambridge student who became vicar of Holy Trinity Church,

Cambridge at the age of twenty-three. Despite opposition from within the parish, the congregation slowly filled up with students; then he introduced an evening service in addition. He was generous in providing hospitality especially for his 'conversation parties' to teach candidates for the ministry to preach. When Simeon died it is estimated that he had taught nearly half of all Anglican ministers in England. He helped with others to establish the London Jews Society, the British and Foreign Bible Society but also the Church Missionary Society.

No wonder that Charles and Mayor were excited to receive the invitation to spend the summer period with a well-known Anglican curate like John Newton. Both students eventually arrived at Olney on the 12 July 1777; for twelve weeks they enjoyed hospitality and fellowship with the Newtons as well as with those attending church services. On the 16 October they returned to Oxford for Charles' final year of studies.

'Very profitable'

In his *Diary* on returning to Oxford, Charles wrote that, 'the visit proved … very profitable indeed.' Writing again in his *Diary* but in early August while still in Olney, he detailed his impressions and the benefits of being with John Newton. One important fact was the excellent teaching he received from Newton's preaching, whose 'edifying discourses' were grounding him well in the Bible. There were also 'conversations' with Newton in the home which were valuable and enlightening. Without exaggeration, Charles asks: 'What place or situation can I be in, more pleasing and delightful?' Then he explains that before arriving in Olney, he recognised that Newton was an important and gifted man 'but really', he acknowledges, 'he has exceeded my … expectations.' In expressing a wish urging his friend Watts Wilkinson to visit them in Olney, he writes: 'I wish you would, I am sure you would like both the shepherd and the sheep...'[1] The 'sheep' here refers to the 'poor simple-hearted Christians' in the congregation at Olney who 'pretend to know nothing but a little of their own hearts and the way of salvation through Christ'. For Charles it was a privilege to fellowship with such believers and he adds: 'There is something pleasing and comfortable in the very sight of those with whom you hope to spend a happy eternity. That my lot may fall among them here and hereafter, is the very utmost of my wishes.'

Another privilege for the students was that Newton's friend, William Romaine was in Olney preaching for two days. It was 'no small pleasure' for Charles to meet and hear Romaine preach for he 'gave us two very excellent sermons on Christ's glory in his person and offices, and on his preciousness to a ruined sinner, when he is enabled to lay hold on him through faith'.[2] Charles then referred to Romaine's preaching claiming it had 'vastly delighted' him. The preaching was distinctive and easy to follow so the uneducated could understand the message. The content of the message too was 'excellent indeed' but 'delivered in such a feeling ... that even my cold, hard heart could not but be warmed a little with his fire'. Such preaching made a huge impression on the young Charles and yet his own feeling of inadequacy to preach was exposed. The strongest physical health coupled with extensive learning, whether secular or sacred, 'would be much too little', he confesses, 'to make me a gospel preacher'. Even eloquence and orthodox beliefs without 'a little of the unction of the Holy Spirit' means that a preacher may 'as well be silent'. In his prayers, studies and meditations, he expressed the

1 ·DEJ, 1, 50-1.
2 DEJ, 1, 43-4.

desire that God would give him and his friends 'a great share of' the anointing of the Holy Spirit when he would be preaching publicly.

Another friendship

While in Olney during the summer of 1777, the two students would have heard about the Rev. Thomas Scott (1747–1821), a curate near Olney. Scott rejected the foundational doctrines of the Bible and tried to engage John Newton in controversy concerning these doctrines. Newton's response surprised Scott for instead of debating doctrine, Newton provided him with spiritual guidance and encouragement with no intention of arguing. Following a period of silence on Scott's part, he again approached Newton but this time to seek spiritual help. From April 1777 until the autumn, Newton counselled him, then Scott was converted. Newton may have shared details of Scott's spiritual pilgrimage with Charles and Mayor while they were in Olney, but in God's providence a friendship between Scott and Charles was established, resulting in Scott supporting Charles for years in varied aspects of his future work. Scott himself became influential within the Church Missionary Society and Scott's Bible Commentary (1792) became very popular amongst Christians.

Oxford and beyond

During the final months in Oxford, Charles' ordination as a curate the following June (1778) was uppermost in his mind. He needed to complete his studies successfully but also prepare himself spiritually for ordination; then there was the question where he would serve as curate. D. E. Jenkins states that Charles 'was already on the look-out for a curacy', and one important reason was his eagerness 'to be independent of his home supplies, and to cease adding to his debt'.[3] During this period, correspondence between Charles and Newton was encouraging. Newton and his wife had missed their guests, Charles and Mayor; the latter 'felt loath to part' when they left Olney for Oxford and they were missed by their hosts. Referring to the office and work of a minister, Newton reminded Charles and Mayor that a minister was no 'superior Being' immune from sin or snares. There will always be the need to continue learning about oneself and the work while maintaining dependence on the Lord. If we do not pray, Newton insisted, whatever gifts we may have, we will be 'but empty and broken cisterns', unable to do what is right and fruitful. It was necessary advice.

Early in 1778 there were frustrations when the possibility of a curacy in Northamptonshire and Worcester under good men fell through. Concerning the closed door in the Worcester curacy, Charles wrote submissively to a friend:

It seems to me that the Angel of the Lord, with his sword drawn in his hand, obstructs my way to Worcester. The will of the Lord be done. I have reason to be thankful for this grace among many others – that I have no choice at all of my own. I hope to follow the fiery, cloudy pillar wherever it may lead; then, though the way may be unknown to me, I am secure, and beyond the possibility of erring out of the right path.

In late March, Charles received and accepted the offer of a curacy in the parishes of Shepton Beauchamp and Sparkford in Somerset. Completing his studies, there was his ordination. Charles wrote in his *Diary*:

---

3 D.E.J, 1, 66-7.

On June 14, 1778, I was ordained Deacon at Oxford. Felt an earnest desire that the Lord would enable me to devote myself wholly to his Service the remainder of my days on Earth; was not a little impressed with a sense of the great importance of the charge I had taken upon me, and of my very great inability to discharge it faithfully and in a due manner. May the Spirit of the Lord Jehovah be upon me evermore.[4]

A few days later reflecting on his ordination, he writes these searching words:

…this is the most awful and most solemn time I have as yet lived to see. My anxious thoughts … and the weighty work I am engaged in, frequently oppresses my spirit very much… Acts xx.28, sounds in my ears day and night. Is the church so dear and precious to Christ that he purchased it with his most precious blood? What bowels of compassion and mercy then should I exercise towards everyone, even the meanest individual? How anxious about their salvation? May God of his infinite goodness enable me to be faithful. At the same time it comforts my heart when I reflect on God's gracious dealings with me, in making it my continual employ, my vocation, to think and speak about the astonishing scheme of salvation, and the glorious author of it. What theme more sweet and ravishing! What topic more spiritual and sublime! Let my heart and tongue, and every member I have, join with St. Paul and all the angels in heaven in glorying in the cross of Christ, and be determined to know nothing else.

With these feelings and thoughts, he looked forward prayerfully to commencing his ministry in Somerset in late September.

---

4   DEJ, 1, 80-2.

Summer months

How would he spend the intervening summer months? His university friend, Simon Lloyd, was from Bala so on Simon's invitation, he and Simon decided to travel in North Wales for five weeks including a few days' stay with Simon's family who were well-known Christians in Bala. Here he also met Sarah Jones though everyone called her Sally. He had admired her from a distance for several years. In addition to meeting the Lloyd family and their friends, there were other highlights during this visit to Wales. He attended the 'Methodist' preaching meetings in Caernarfonshire then heard two sermons from Daniel Rowland in Llangeitho at a Methodist Association on their way to spend the rest of the summer break with Charles' family in Carmarthenshire. Charles also preached for the first time in mid-August where, he writes, 'My heart exceedingly rejoiced to see once more my old very dear friend Rees Hugh. I could almost have cried for joy.' But it was the last time for them to meet for his friend died a month later.

The summer months went by quickly and near the end of September he wrote to a friend from Somerset. He had been there only for one week and admits that preaching, 'is hard work' but the Lord's promise to be with him, he declared, 'is all my comfort and support; and indeed I want no more.' Growing opposition to his preaching, a reducing salary and the considerable distance between the two churches he pastored required him to find comfort in the Lord. Charles refused an offer of a curacy in Buckinghamshire on the ground that 'an all-wise Providence' had placed him in that difficult situation. Despite being lonely when 'Providence appears dark and mysterious … I am strongly persuaded God sent me here: for what end it does not yet appear very clear.'

However, there were encouragements for Charles. His friend Simon Lloyd had accepted a curacy near Bristol which encouraged Charles, even though it involved 'a morning's ride' to visit him. Charles also established a close friendship with John Lucas, vicar of Milborne Port whose parish was reasonably near where Simon Lloyd served. Charles and Lucas agreed to meet for a couple of days every third week for fellowship and prayer. Lucas required assistance too in his parish so he gave Charles a small amount of money for his help to cover reductions in his salary. Despite these encouragements and the fact that Charles' parishioners were civil towards him, they had 'a very great contempt of the gospel and godly living'.

Was there a more responsive church where his preaching and pastoral work would be welcomed? That is the theme of the next two chapters, but Charles was beginning to feel the need of a godly wife. The Lord in His providence would provide and that is the theme of the next chapter.

5 Romance

———————————————————●

A romance! And a happy ending but only eventually! Aspects of this romance are fascinating and unusual so the following questions and answers may help explain the development and importance of the romance, then marriage, for Charles' future ministry.

Questions

Q: Who was the young lady?

A: We noted earlier she was Sally Jones (1753–1814) from Bala, North Wales, the only child of David and Jane Jones who had a busy family grocery and drapery business in the town where Sally also helped. The family were financially comfortable due to the income from their shop and they could afford to employ servants to assist in the home and shop. Her father died when she was six years of age, then her mother remarried two years later. The stepfather was Thomas Foulkes (1731–1802), a Christian whom Sally came to love dearly. Foulkes had been deeply influenced by John Wesley's Arminianism [1] but nevertheless settled well in the Calvinistic Methodist fellowship

---

1   Foulkes advocated Arminian teaching openly in the later years of his life after remarrying and settling in Machynlleth.

in Bala. Foulkes' responsibility was to manage the shop, but Sally began to assume more responsibility in her teens which released her stepfather to undertake additional preaching in the rural, farming areas. Bala's small population gradually increased, partly due to its woollen industry making the town relatively important in North Wales.

Q: How did Charles meet Sally?

A: He did not meet her for about five years after first hearing of her. The story starts when he was studying in Carmarthen Academy when he sometimes heard local Christians in the society share news about the Lord's work in Wales, including Bala, so Sally's name was occasionally mentioned. She and her family were widely known and respected for their love of the Lord and involvement in the Bala Methodist Society. He was impressed by what he heard about her. To his friend Edward Griffin, in October 1780, he wrote: 'You must know that I have had a young lady in view *some years past,* with whom I intended, should the will of heaven be so, forming a matrimonial connection … I never should have thought of her had I not been fully persuaded that she travelled the same road…'[2]

One can only imagine the delight Charles must have felt when his student friend from Bala, Simon Lloyd, suggested that following completion of his studies in Oxford and after his ordination as an Anglican Deacon, he should visit Bala for a holiday in the summer of 1778. It was here he was able to meet Sally for the first time, though it was brief and she was not swept off her feet by him! He was convinced Sally was 'born of God'. Although she was attractive in appearance, it was not physical attraction that impressed him the

---

2 Richard Bennett 'Letters of Thomas Charles', *Journal of the Historical Society of the Presbyterian Church of Wales*, vol. 5, (1920), p. 39. (Abbreviated later to JHS)

most but her strong Christian character and love for the Lord. That was precisely what he wanted in his future wife.[3] Following that low-key meeting, he wrote to a trusted friend: 'I could not have thought it possible I ever should have met with a person so perfectly agreeable to *me* in *everything*.'

Q: What happened following their initial meeting in Bala?

A: Nothing much, at least for a year or more. Months after the visit, he informed Simon Lloyd: 'I think sometimes of Miss Jones,' but he remained undecided about approaching her directly and immediately. By 22 November 1779, after receiving more information about Sally, he confessed to his friend: 'I frequently think of her.' By the end of December that year, he had taken the plunge and written to Sally, addressing her as 'My very dear friend'. His letter was honest and to the point. He shared how she was constantly in his thoughts and 'what secret pleasure and joy' he had known in meeting her months previously. He referred to her wisdom, beauty, modesty and piety which only increased his desire to meet her again. In case she imagined he was flattering her or wanting a share of her wealth, Charles added: 'You are the only person that ever I saw … with whom I thought I could spend my life in happy union and felicity…' Once again Charles refers to the Lord's providence in this matter. The Lord's will was of great importance to him.

Q: Did Sally respond?

A: Yes, but a month later, addressing him as 'Reverend Sir'. She emphasised she was settled in Bala with her family and not enthusiastic about corresponding with Charles. In fact, she suggested

---

3 Eifion Evans aptly described Sally as, 'a woman of exceptional qualities, shrewd in financial affairs and mature in spiritual matters, attractive and intelligent'; *Bread of Heaven*, p. 313.

he may not want to write to her again after reading her initial reply. His letter to her was shown to her parents who held Charles in high esteem.

Q: How did Charles respond and develop the relationship?

A: He replied quickly to Sally's letter on the 27 January 1780, addressing her now as 'My dearest friend'.[4] He had been nervous opening her letter but 'greedily devoured every word in it'. He recognised she was dubious concerning his motives, but he stressed he was sincere in his intentions towards her. His statement that 'I never will or *can think* of anyone else, whilst there remains the *least* prospect of succeeding with you', may have moved Sally deeply. His affection for her was not 'a momentary impulse on unsteady passions'. He ended the letter with words based on 2 Corinthians chapter 1 verses 3-6: 'May *the Father of mercies* bless you with *all* spiritual blessings in Christ, and comfort you with all the rich consolations of the Spirit.' He continued in encouraging Sally and himself by urging: 'Let us not be dismayed, for our gracious, *tender Father* has already engaged all the attributes of the Godhead to see us more than conquerors over all our enemies.'

Q: In which ways did Charles help Sally in her doubts?

A: 'Reverend Sir' was again the respectful way Sally addressed Charles in her second letter of the 14 February but it was with reluctance she had written. However, Sally now began to share her fear of death and lack of assurance that she was a genuine believer.

Charles responded in his third letter (1 March), sharing that he had also known similar fears of death. However, for him, 'That Scripture, 1 Corinthians 15:25-26, was remarkably blessed to me for the removing of all the very alarming and anxious thoughts about

---

4 DEJ, 1, 148-50.

death, which till then deprived me of lasting comfort… I saw I had nothing to do but enjoy the victory, Christ is engaged to conquer. The victory is obtained by the arm of omnipotence…'[5]

Sally's response (16 March) was predictable. She did not deserve Charles' attention and the possibility of marriage was 'at some great distance' and 'as a thing never to come to pass…' What comforted her was that 'the wheel of Providence is in a good hand… If we had to turn it for ourselves … we are often blind to our own happiness, and seek it where it is least to be found…' Like Charles, providence was hugely important to her, for she viewed her life, circumstances and future through the lens of God's wise, good and controlling providence. Her lack of assurance was evident again, while for this, and other reasons, she insists their correspondence be confidential; she agreed to Charles' suggestion they should disguise their handwriting on the envelope to avoid gossip in the Bala Post Office!

Charles himself was busy settling into church work in Milborne Port in Somerset where he would 'assist' the vicar. He felt settled by early April, and Sally's letter (27 April) expressed her satisfaction with this, but with the accompanying reminder that his success in ministry depended on 'the power and faithfulness of God'. She shared with him her own spiritual need, like 'lukewarmness and deadness', with her fervent longing for the 'cheering warming influence of the Sun of righteousness to dissolve the hardness' of her heart. Sally knew the answer to her need: 'A view of redeeming love. Jesus dying on the Cross is the most powerful quickening, … in Jesus there is all fulness.' Nor should Charles feel obliged to continue the correspondence. In late April, Charles sent Sally, on impulse, some poetry which he had found helpful in a magazine sometime previously. It was intended

---

5 DEJ, 1, 156-8.

as a 'memento' to remind her of his care and 'expectations'. But Sally was 'surprised', troubled and mystified by the poetry so she wrote requesting an explanation. Their letters crossed, for Charles had also written to her expressing sympathy for her spiritual need, agreeing that she had 'certainly found, … and pointed me to it, a view of redeeming love – Jesus dying on the Cross' as the 'effectual remedy' for spiritual difficulties in Christian experience. He was also glad to hear of the success of the 'everlasting Gospel' in Bala. A significant part of the letter, however, stressed his love and esteem for her, so he did not want to end the correspondence. He waited 'for nothing but a concurrence of sentiments in you on the point' of future marriage. Charles was persistent in expressing his love but also sensitive in caring pastorally for Sally! The Lord was at the centre of their lives and relationship. Was it God's will they should marry? Sally was unconvinced, for she was settled with her parents in Bala and they needed her in the family business so she felt constrained to remain in Bala supporting them.

Q: Did Charles show wisdom handling this correspondence?
A: On the whole he did, but on occasions he lacked wisdom and sensitivity, particularly in two early situations. While slow progress was being made in the relationship, he was thrilled to receive the first unexpected letter from Sally and read of her 'ardent wishes' that the Lord would sustain him in his situation. He read her letter many times with great pleasure and replied quickly calling her 'my dear, dearest friend'. Charles described the background to the poetry he had sent her, apologising for giving her a feeling of unease about it. 'I indeed meant nothing at all by sending' the poetry, 'but to induce you to write to me', and then admits, 'when writing to you I do not know when to stop.' He signed off the letter with the words, 'Your

most affectionate and unchangeable friend and humble servant'.[6]
Sally's response dated 12 May reported, 'the great revival of religion
in South Wales … and some clergymen in South Wales are … made
flaming ministers of the sanctuary' yet the work in Bala remained at
a standstill. Interestingly, she signed the letter as 'your affectionate
friend and scrawler'!

Ahead of Charles now was his ordination as priest in Oxford on
the 21 May. It was a solemn occasion for him. In his *Diary*, he records
his prayer and longings as he began his ministry:

O Almighty God who has given me the will, grant also power to
perform the same, accomplish the work you have begun in me –
endow me with a double portion of Thy Spirit and clothe me with
power from on high – increase my love to souls – impress my mind
deeply and constantly with a sense of the solemn account I must
one day render to Thee of my stewardship – enable me to exercise
the gifts given me – lift up my hands whenever they hang down
and strengthen my feeble knees – help me to be in Thy hands as
the clay in the hands of the Potter, willing to be ruled, fashioned
and employed by Thy godly wisdom in the manner and for the
service Thou thinkest proper – I am nothing in myself – mine eyes
are directed unto Thee in whom the fatherless find mercy – O never
leave me – Thou art a faithful God who never failed those who
depend upon Thee.

Following his ordination, Charles shared his prayer with Sally, with
a plea for her prayers: 'The Lord it seems will always put his rich
treasures in earthen vessels that the glory may be entirely his.' He
explained that Sally, 'is at all times nearest my heart and … never
absent from me, whether I am holding conversation with heaven,

---

6   DEJ, 1, 176-9

or earth … you are equally present with me, to recommend you to the favour and protection of' the Lord. Her response was cautious but expresses again her uncertainty that she was a Christian, yet encouragingly for Charles, admitted: 'I love to pour my complaints to you because I believe you think of me at the throne of grace… I sometimes attempt to commit you to Him that intercedes for you.'

He was unwise in pressurising Sally. Addressing her in his next letter as 'My dearest Love', he says he informed friends of his engagement to a young lady. He also wanted permission to visit her in Bala, but Sally was not pleased! In a formal reply she did not want to hear about an engagement and would 'rather converse … at a distance … than have a personal discourse with you…' in Bala.

Q: Was the door being shut for Charles?

A: It seemed so but correspondence during July marked an improvement in tone from Sally. Charles emphasised he wanted to see her in Bala and was willing to 'come as an acquaintance' of the Lloyd family if necessary but 'you must absolutely promise me very frequent interviews with you during my stay there.' Charles was insistent. Sally's letter to Charles dated 17 July assured him she had no reason for avoiding him when he visited Bala, for the visit in the Lord's providence may make clear the purpose for them having corresponded. She later offered him accommodation as the family had 'never refused a bed to any that have asked' (9 August). Her family was renowned for extending hospitality to visitors, including itinerant preachers and Charles and Sally continued this custom after their marriage.

The four-day journey to Bala on horseback started on 4 September. Charles was excited for this was only the second time for him to see Sally and visit Bala. Sally was probably apprehensive, but any positive feelings she had for Charles were suppressed by shyness, doubts and low self-esteem. On his long journey, he 'experienced a Spirit of prayer, that the Lord would be with me, comfort me with his presence, support me by his power and direct me with his Holy Spirit – preventing me from taking any step without consulting him and knowing his will – I was also enabled in some degree to believe he would be with me in this important affair. Lord, keep me from following my own will and inclination in it.' The visit to Bala went well; both enjoyed fellowship while Sally's parents were kindly disposed to Charles, holding him in great respect.

A report of the 'long tedious journey' back to Somerset was sent to Sally immediately. His parishioners 'were glad' he had returned. Reflecting on the days in Bala, he was aware of 'many undeserved mercies' he experienced there and especially that Sally 'graciously inclined' her heart towards him, as did her parents. He had never met 'a person so perfectly agreeable' to him 'in everything' but he 'did not want to sin by being impatient waiting for a favourable' marital conclusion to their relationship. His affections for her would never change. Sally responded cautiously but warmly (18 October), feeling relieved that the wet weather throughout Charles' journey home had not made him ill. Concerning the future, she was content with her present circumstances but wanted them both 'to submit to whatever appears to be the will of heaven towards us… If the thing be not from the Lord, may he frustrate the procedure of it, He can do it to our utmost satisfaction. We have no cause to be anxious nor impatient.'

Q: Did Charles understand what falling in love meant for her?
A: Yes, and he began to explain it to her. Sally was becoming more emotionally attached to Charles, more pastorally dependent on him,

and appreciative of his prayer support in her personal struggles. He was 'the first' she had shared these struggles with. Charles was more encouraged in pursuing the relationship and talks about love, then marriage. His letter of 18 November gave relevant advice. Addressing Sally as 'My Dear, Dearest Heart', he makes some important points about falling in love. He emphasised first, that passions and feelings are unreliable and changing so they cannot be relied upon. No marriage survives if based solely on physical attraction. Second, conviction is needed and 'likely to be lasting' but this conviction needs to be grounded in God's Word, confirmed by providence so the conviction gives passion its proper place. Thirdly, in expressing his heart and love towards Sally, he wanted to prioritise encouraging each other in faith and love towards the Lord 'to whom we are under such infinite obligations…' The Lord must be at the centre of their courtship and marriage. To reinforce the point, he emphasised the words: 'Christ died for the ungodly' (Romans 5: 6), telling Sally:

> I love to repeat the words, because all my hopes and comforts in time and eternity are grounded upon them. I am not afraid to depend on this foundation – I am sure it will never fail… Well then, 'Christ died for the ungodly'; is not this enough? O let us no longer doubt but believe in him, love him, delight in him, and set forth his praise not only with our lips but in our lives!

He was encouraging Sally in her lack of Christian assurance but also, he highlighted the need for courting/married couples to be Christ-centred and to revel in the undeserved mercy and grace of God. That could only serve to strengthen and sanctify their relationship. A week later on the 25 November he writes to her about marriage! The Rev. John Newton heard he was considering marriage so he wrote to encourage Charles. For Newton, marriage, if 'put under the management of faith, prayer and prudence is a happy business'. There are advantages of a minister being married, especially in understanding and sympathising with people in their different family and personal needs. Charles was clear concerning both love and marriage.

Q: How did Charles resolve the problem of location?

A: He was persistent and prayed much about it! He was in love, convinced he should marry Sally, whatever the difficulties but he longed for the Lord's providence to confirm this. He knew it would be difficult for Sally to leave Bala and the family. Sally too did not want to hinder Charles from serving wherever the Lord placed him for he could obtain a good church in England or in South Wales. Many Anglicans would frown upon the fact she was a 'Methodist'. They struggled therefore with their correspondence having its peaks and lows. Charles persisted despite the disappointing months from early 1781 until autumn 1782 when he was unable to obtain a suitable curacy near Bala.

Providence slowly became clearer for Charles, although initially he felt inclined to accept the attractive offer of a curacy in Llangan, near Bridgend in South Wales on the recommendation of Rev. John Newton. The Rev. David Jones had been ordained as an Anglican clergyman in 1760 and, after serving other parishes, settled in Llangan near Bridgend in 1767 having been profoundly influenced by reading John Flavel's *Works*. Jones was a gifted preacher and many people flocked to his parish church to hear him preach. Eifion Evans explains that 'Llangan became the counterpart in South Wales of Llangeitho in mid-Wales, a vigorous centre of Methodist witness.'[7]

---

7 *Bread of Heaven*, 208. William Williams, Pantycelyn referred to him as 'honest Jones of Llan-gan' whose 'orthodoxy was sound and reliable'.

Although it was an attractive opportunity for Charles to serve in Llangan, he was shaken to hear from Sally (21 February 1781) that this would mean 'a final separation between us' for she did not want to be a 'hindrance'. The letter was difficult for Sally to write but Charles immediately declined the offer of the curacy because he longed to be with Sally. His concern for her deepened when her letter (21 June 1781) reported she had almost died returning to Bala from a fair in a nearby village when a sudden but violent storm developed. Sally struggled through water, ditches and often scrambled on to firm ground near hedges for somewhere safe to stand. In the end she found a house where she was welcomed. Knowing Sally was discouraged that no curacy had become available closer to Bala, he arranged to visit her to talk through issues and it proved helpful, though the future remained uncertain for them.

Q: What did Charles do to resolve the dilemma?
A: There was very little he could do, but his illness from exhaustion at the end of 1781 challenged Charles. In mid-January 1782 he wrote in his *Diary* that the Lord had brought about 'a very great deliverance' for his soul after a difficult year. The main lesson he learned was the need to be patient and trust the Lord for his marriage and its timing. Consequently, he found himself 'very submissive and resigned to God's will concerning me and all my affairs', especially his marriage to Sally which had 'engaged my heart and affections for these two past years'.

Q: Did he find it easy to be patient and submissive?
A: Not really because he found separation from Sally intolerable. Their correspondence continued and because of 'the unhappy distance from each other' (15 March 1782), their letters were essential as they

shared and prayed for one another. The many months almost until their wedding on the 20 August 1783 was a strain for them, especially as Charles endeavoured to find work near Bala while continuing his ministry in Somerset. He felt frustrated.

Q: What did he do?

A: He took the initiative and decided to move to Bala! It was a major decision. Was he irresponsible and impetuous? Charles had considered the facts carefully and prayed for many months so he was not being hasty.

Q: Did he have good reasons for this decision?

A: Yes, for he concluded he could just as well serve the Lord near Bala as in Somerset. [8] That was a significant reason for him. And it was a fact, for there was a church a few miles from Bala where he could assist the vicar free of charge until he found his own church. Being in Bala also meant he could apply for any church vacancy which became available in the area. In addition, his replacement for the Somerset church was available which freed him to go to Bala. These were solid reasons informing his decision and which he shared with Sally in his letter of the 28 February 1783. Exciting? Yes, and confirmation came when the rector of the Mallwyd parish church near Bala, wrote on the 5th of May to welcome the possibility of Charles assisting him in ministry there but without salary.

Q: How did Sally respond?

A: As you suspect, she had serious doubts and wrote on the 29th May: '…we have need to be directed from above… I hope we shall be enabled to know and do the will of the Lord… I am not positive nor

8 DEJ, 1, 98-100

confident how it will be… I endeavour to weigh the matter seriously,' then she refers again to her fears and doubts about being a Christian.

Q: Did Charles change his mind?

A: Not at all. His love for Sally and the conviction God was guiding him enabled him to relocate to Bala and marry Sally. Until their wedding three months later, Sally remained doubtful, but he informed Sally, when leaving Somerset (23 June), that he was, 'fully persuaded, be the consequences what it will, it was the will of the Lord I should do so.' [9] He visited friends on the way to Bala, arriving there in mid-July. Their marriage took place on the 20th August 1783 in St Beuno's Church, Llanycil on the outskirts of Bala town. Charles recorded in his *Diary*:

> Every obstacle in the way was abundantly useful, and the delay though to me was exceedingly tedious, was exceedingly beneficial and absolutely necessary… Trials and crosses and disappointments shall be sent to drive them to the throne of grace, to bring them to deny themselves, to be resigned to his sovereign will, and to believe before they possess, in everything they shall live by faith.

Sally too was relieved and became extremely affectionate and supportive of her husband. Letters from her in the autumn to Charles while he was on his preaching journeys expressed her deep love and longings to see him: 'The idea of being reduced to live on letters again is not pleasing. Indeed, I long to see you, and I have a right to live with you *till death us do part.*'

An unusual courtship? Possibly, for it spanned a period of ten years from the day Charles first heard of Sally and he had only seen her on four occasions during that period. Their bonding by means of

---

9   DEJ, 1, 415

correspondence was invaluable as was the strength of Charles' love and care for her. His persistence, patience, gentle pastoral concern with its clear focus on the Lord coupled with an unquestioning acceptance of the Lord's gracious providence were rewarded. Christ was at the centre of this relationship. It was Christ Charles would preach and serve from his new base in Bala with the unflinching support of his wife. That is the story of the next chapters.

6 Bala: A New Ministry

A few days after his marriage in August 1783, Charles wrote to a friend: 'I am now waiting to see what the Lord has to do with me.' Married and settling in Bala as his permanent base, he needed to know where he could serve the Lord's church for it was 'disagreeable and uncomfortable to be doing nothing', especially as he had a passion to preach the gospel of Christ. It was strange as an ordained minister not to be preaching on Sundays and in midweek meetings. In a letter to a friend about five weeks after his marriage, he explained that he had made 'use of every means in my power to procure some employment in the established church', yet not for the sake of obtaining a salary 'but from a principle of conscience... I am a churchman on principle, and therefore shall not on any account leave it, unless I am forced to do so.' [1] He added that he could live independent of the church financially, a reference to his wife's earned income in the family shop.

Once again disappointments lay ahead and a radically different ministry from what he had expected. He was being 'forced' out of

1 DEJ, 1, 427

regular ministry in the state church without realising, and being prepared for a strategic ministry amongst the Calvinistic Methodists. The Lord's guidance was gradual, for Charles was an Anglican by conviction, and it would be a personal struggle for him to be willing to minister exclusively outside the Established Church.

Rejection

One major factor in the Lord's providence at this time was his dismissal from three curacies in different parishes, all in reasonably close proximity to Bala. It was a difficult period of facing fierce opposition from clergy and parishioners. The three curacies were miles apart but the pattern was clear. His clear and forthright biblical preaching was unacceptable to most congregations. One parish church was in Llangynog where he only survived two Sundays. The same happened in a different parish in Llandegla and Bryneglwys where his friend was a vicar. Due to the vicar's illness, Charles was asked to help there but by the second Sunday the parishioners in Llandegla prevented him by force from preaching. In a letter to a friend, Charles wrote: 'What the Lord means to do with me, I know not, but I hope I shall know soon.' [2] He was desperate to know God's plan.

There was, however, an opportunity for him to preach for his friend John Mayor, the vicar in Shawbury, Shropshire, a distance of about fifty miles from Bala. Weekly from October 1783 to January 1784 Charles preached there, staying there each weekend or sometimes longer. It was a ministry Charles appreciated although he and Sally found it difficult being apart. During these weeks he was blessed in his own heart in recognising 'the exceedingly sinfulness of sin' while having 'some glorious views of Christ in his person and offices. More

---

2   DEJ, 1, 426

so than I ever experienced before...' He also highlighted the need to 'be supplied with strength to *work*, but also to be taught continually and directed *how* to work and *where* to work'.

By January, he applied for and obtained a curacy in Llanymawddwy, commencing his ministry there on 24 January 1784. He travelled there weekly on a Saturday and returned to Bala after preaching at the Wednesday morning service. Encouragingly, the people were eager to hear the Word preached and Charles informed his wife in a letter that he had experienced 'a little of the divine presence in preaching last Sunday'. He was sure the Lord had sent him there and that his labours would be blessed. Once again there was opposition but not from the parishioners. Three clergymen in the area schemed to have Charles dismissed, and succeeded, despite a petition from the congregation supporting their curate. His two months of ministry there ended abruptly.

Charles tried hard to get other opportunities for parish ministry in North Wales but to no avail. Doors seemed to be closed to him with many Anglicans in North Wales suspecting him of being a 'Methodist'.

Unhelpful advice

Charles was learning more about the importance of humility and patience. He wrote:

> Our progress in the divine life is always safely estimated by our progress in humility. Humility is the strength and ornament of all other graces; it is the food that nourishes them; the soil in which they grow.

He felt frustrated and impatient in not securing a church ministry. It was a trial but, 'I hope this will teach me humility...' in bending to the Lord's will in all that happened in his life and circumstances. In one letter[3] he shared honestly: 'I am in a strait between two things – between leaving the church and continuing in it.[4] The question arose acutely for him: 'What shall I do? Christ's words continually sound in my ears, "Feed my lambs." I feel my heart willing to engage in the work, be the consequences what they may…' but decides he should 'wait a little longer to see what the Lord will do'.

A friend had shared with the Rev. John Newton in Olney the frustrations Charles felt in not obtaining a curacy near Bala. A letter duly reached him from Newton (26 June 1784), urging him not to leave the Established Church but to use his gifts and abilities within parish churches. There were ample opportunities to serve in England where his preaching and pastoral work would be greatly valued. Newton had not understood Sally's conflict and commitments in caring for her parents and their business as well as supporting her husband financially, so Newton asked Charles whether it was a mere convenience to live in Bala and near to Sally? Newton went further. He suggested that, 'the Lord has permitted you to be silenced in Wales may be that he has a work for you to do in Yorkshire or Northumberland…' Was the Lord speaking or could a famous man like John Newton be wrong? Charles felt Newton's advice was unhelpful, so there was a greater need to humbly seek the Lord's will. There were reasons why Charles should reject Newton's advice. His heart was in Wales. Further, when leaving Somerset for the last time, he informed Sally he was 'fully persuaded' whatever the consequences that it was the Lord's will to leave for Bala and settle there. He had wrestled with the question for a long period and reached that settled conviction. Now married, providentially his

3 June 12, 1784

4 DEJ, 1, 490

family circumstances tied him even more closely to Bala and Wales. Newton's advice, however, compelled him to think more about his future ministry for he felt locked in providence. There was more for him to learn.

Exciting!

Charles was learning more about the exciting background to the Bala Society – one in which Howell Harris had a significant part. Although commencing studies in Oxford, Harris only remained there one week because his burden for evangelism was overwhelming, with the Lord blessing him extensively in his exhorting and preaching, locally and nationally. With Daniel Rowland, Howell Davies, William Williams of Pantycelyn, Harris was one of four leaders of the major revival in Wales from the mid-1730s. Emerging within the revival, the Calvinistic Methodist movement operated strictly within the Anglican Church but it was evangelical, Calvinistic and influenced by the Westminster Confession of Faith; it was also dynamic and experiential. They deliberately used the term 'society' for their meetings in order to emphasise they were not a church. Their leaders too were nearly all lay exhorters, but the movement expanded significantly between 1739 and 1745 when more societies were formed and regular conferences or 'associations' were arranged for supervising society activities. In 1743 Harris was appointed 'Superintendent' of all these societies for a brief period.

Harris' first two visits to Bala were in 1740 (13 February and 3 November) when he preached to hundreds of people, despite opposition. For Harris' third visit[5] in November 1741, the rector of Llanycil Church had organised a mob to attack and hinder him from

---

5 Howell Harris visited Bala later in 1747, 1748 and 1749, resulting in more conversions and the strengthening of believers in the society.

preaching. Crowds greeted his arrival with laughter and ridicule. He preached in the street but withdrew to the safety of a home where he felt the Lord's power in preaching. Windows in the house were shattered by the mob until Harris left to face his persecutors before running away from them. However, they caught up with him, beating him mercilessly for some time. This incident was probably the worst physical attack he suffered as the men and women hit him with their fists and sticks. They dragged him bleeding out of town close to the lake and the parish church of Llanycil. In a remarkable providence, the Lord enabled Harris to escape, yet despite such vicious attacks during this visit, people were converted through his preaching.

By 1745 the society was formed in Bala with eight members,[6] one of whom included John Evans who became a prominent member and exhorter. Sally's mother was also an early convert of Harris and member of this society. John Evans (1723–1817) deserves more attention. Born in the Wrexham area of North-East Wales, he had received a reasonably good education, but from the age of twelve he was apprenticed as a weaver for three years. Without work afterwards, he was unsettled for a period before having a temporary job, until a difficult situation made him leave and look for employment as far as possible from North Wales. In search for employment, the teenager heard of vacancies in Cardigan, West Wales, so he decided to go there. There was one problem: he had no idea where Cardigan was or how to reach the town! On his way there, he stopped in Bala in May 1742, en route for Cardigan, but providentially he settled in the town because accommodation and work became available to him immediately. He also began attending a meeting of Methodists, for it was held in his employer's home. That fellowship was significant for

---

6 By 1752 there were over twenty members in the Bala Society.

him and in 1745 Evans was converted. He became a faithful member, exhorter and leader in the Bala Society for several decades. John Evans became a gifted preacher.[7] Several months before their marriage, Sally wrote to Charles to report on Evans' preaching: 'I never heard the Captain of our Salvation set out more lovely than at that time…' while Charles responded generously: 'I know no one whom I could hear with more real profit and satisfaction next to the great Rowlands himself…' Evans and Charles became close friends and co-workers. In 1747, the first Calvinistic Methodist chapel was built in the town.[8] John Evans' influence and role in Bala and in the area was hugely significant: 'Mr John Evans of Bala was mighty in the Scriptures, firm and steadfast in upholding the principles of the Christian religion. He stood as a faithful witness for the truth, in doctrine and discipline, for the unusually long period of seventy-five years.'[9]

Robert Jones, Rhos-lan

Events now moved quickly for Thomas Charles. After receiving John Newton's discouraging letter, and while his wife Sally was away in Chester on business, Charles attended the weekly society meeting where his wife and her parents were members, with Thomas Foulkes being an important lay preacher there. Years previously as a teenager he had attended the local Methodist Society in Carmarthen where he enjoyed hearing believers share their experiences of the Lord.

---

7 P. Owen *Atgofion John Evans y Bala: Y Diwygiad Methodistaidd ym Meirionnydd a Mon,* Golgwyd gan Goronwy (Caernarfon: Gwasg Pantycelyn, 1997).

8 The chapel building in Bala was extended in 1782 and 1792; a new chapel building was erected in 1809.

9 'History of the Calvinistic Methodists' in *The History, Constitution, Rules and Discipline and Confession of Faith of the Calvinist Methodists or the Presbyterian Church of Wales,* Published by the General Assembly, (revised edition 1900, Caernarfon).

For Charles as a convinced churchman, in going to the local society meeting he was not abandoning the Anglican Church or its ministry, for the Calvinistic Methodists worshipped in Anglican churches regularly, observed the sacraments there and were married and buried by the church.

That evening he was greatly encouraged in listening to Robert Jones (1745–1829), the leader of the Calvinistic Methodists in North Wales. Born in Caernarfonshire, Jones had attended one of Griffith Jones's circulating schools and became a teacher in those schools for several years. He began to exhort in 1768 among the Calvinistic Methodists, quickly becoming a prominent leader and preacher. Under Robert Jones's preaching that evening, Charles was greatly helped, experiencing considerable joy as he worshipped the triune God with others. He longed to share this news with Sally when she returned home.

It is likely that Charles and Robert Jones that evening shared details regarding their respective ministries and situations, with Jones aware of Charles' availability for ministry, for the Calvinistic Methodists had a desperate need for preachers in North Wales. Until then, their chapels and societies in the North had largely depended on clergy and lay preachers from the South ministering to them at regular intervals. By 1784 there were forty-seven of their chapels/societies meeting weekly in the North but scattered through Anglesey, Caernarfonshire, Merioneth, Radnorshire, Denbighshire and Flintshire. Who would care for them? The need was urgent. Was the Lord opening a new door for Charles? His availability and such desperate needs of care for the scattered Methodists were factors making the Lord's providence clearer for him.

Decision time

Charles had little to do apart from helping in the family business, but his heart was in ministry. Becoming aware of poor, uneducated children in the town, he felt compelled to help, so he held a school in his home, but very soon the number of children attending increased so their home became too small. The Methodist chapel had been extended in 1782 and it was agreed Charles could use the premises for a school. In this way closer links were established resulting in Christians urging him to minister the Word amongst them. The pressure was considerable and providence indicated that while parish churches were closed to him, another door opened where he was desperately needed.

Charles' mind was made up. During the summer of 1784, only a year after his marriage, he became a member of the Methodist Society in Bala. After his acceptance, he travelled to Llangeitho where the Methodist Association was meeting for fellowship and preaching; here he was formally accepted as a clergyman amongst the Methodists. Within weeks, Charles was busy visiting groups of Methodists in North-West Wales and itinerant preaching would now be a permanent feature of his ministry in addition to other demands. There was no doubt where his future ministry lay.

But don't miss the big picture: Charles became the first clergyman in North Wales who gave himself wholly to minister amongst the Calvinistic Methodists. The Lord's plan was being unfolded.

7 'The Lord's Gift'

———————————————————————•

After hearing the Rev. Thomas Charles preach in Llangeitho in the summer of 1785, Daniel Rowland remarked: 'Charles is the Lord's gift to the North.' That was true. Charles' Christian experience, gifts, training, as well as his Anglican credentials, made him invaluable in pastoring Calvinistic Methodists. Through all the twists and turns, the Lord had prepared him; he was 'the Lord's gift' now urgently needed in the North but also elsewhere.

Impact of revivals

Charles began his itinerant preaching in North Wales during autumn 1784 and quickly appreciated the impact of recent revivals in the area. There was the 1762–1764 revival in Llangeitho which R. Geraint Gruffydd described as, 'perhaps the first distinct, fairly widespread revival in Welsh Methodist history'.[1] Eifion Evans suggested the revival could be aptly described as a 'deluge of grace,'[2] in which a

---

1 Emyr Roberts and R. Geraint Gruffydd 'The Revival of 1762 and William Williams of Pantycelyn' in *Revival & Its Fruit,* (Bridgend: Evangelical Library of Wales, 1981), p. 19.

2 'Deluge' was a word used first in this context by William Williams, Pantycelyn to describe the exceptional power evident under the preaching of

greater degree of the Spirit's power and influence was known by the preacher and congregation. The difference on such occasions is one of degree, not quality. For the same Holy Spirit who regenerates, indwells, sanctifies and strengthens each Christian, sovereignly works more powerfully and extensively through the Word. This is what is meant by 'revival', though the 'ordinary', ongoing work of the Holy Spirit continues, for no one can become or remain a Christian apart from the Holy Spirit. Christians in Wales believed it was biblical to seek God in prayer for a greater degree of the Holy Spirit's power.

There was a background of prayer to the 1762 Llangeitho revival, but also broken relationships between leaders were in the process of being restored. William Williams took his new collection of hymns to Llangeitho and they were sung with joy by those revelling in the grace of God in Christ. In addition, Daniel Rowland had just been forced out of his curacy in Llangeitho parish church. What happened in this revival? Drawing on the oral testimony of those present, Robert Jones of Rhos-lan reported that in 1762:

> In the face of great unworthiness and baseness, God remembered his covenant, by visiting graciously a great number of sinners in several parts of Wales… I heard from a godly old woman that it lasted three days and three nights without a break in a place called Lon-fudr in Lleyn, Caernarfonshire, one crowd following the other … although they went to their homes for a while, they could stay there hardly any time before returning. When these powerful outpourings descended on several hundreds, if not thousands, throughout South Wales and Gwynedd, there arose much excitement and controversy.'[3]

Howell Davies.

3 *Revival & Its Fruit*, pp. 21-2

The singing, even jumping and dancing, attracted attention and criticism, but many people were soundly converted, rejoicing in salvation with a new love and zeal for the Lord. Some of these converts Charles met on his early journeys in North Wales.

There was also the general revival during the years 1778–1782 which affected North Wales and other parts of Wales. During a Bala Association meeting in June 1781, a greater degree of blessing was experienced, which Sally had reported to Charles. In North Caernarfonshire in the village of Clynnog, Richard Dafydd was empowered in preaching, although a very ordinary preacher. Numbers of people were converted under his preaching over a period of time. During the early months of his itinerant preaching, Charles himself preached in the Lleyn Peninsula at Lon Fudr where Thomas Jones (1756–1820) reported that, 'his sermon was with power and acceptance so remarkable, that its fragrance filled that district, and spread also to the country around.' Charles was moving amongst Christians deeply affected by revival, and unsurprisingly, his own preaching was also powerful and fruitful.

Months previously, while assisting in a parish church in Shropshire in January 1784, Charles wrote to his wife:

'Help me, my dear, with your fervent prayers… I long to see past times of the outpouring of the Spirit returning again, when the voice of God by his ministers was terrible, powerful and full of majesty.'

That prayer had been answered partly and Charles was witnessing the Lord working in North Wales, even under his own preaching. There was greater blessing and gospel progress ahead for him. On the opening day of 1785, Charles was able to write:

When I reflect upon the last year, I see great cause for thankfulness … the Lord has in some degree blessed my poor ministerial labours. I never found Satan so busy tempting me to unfaithfulness in my Master's service, since I have been in orders. It surprised me much… In the course of the last year I met with several trials of different natures – but not one that was not wanted … but worked together for good. The Lord's principal design in them all seemed to be the mortification of a worldly spirit within me… My prayer this day is, 'Take not thy Holy Spirit from me,' but this year work more glorious than ever in me and by me to the glory of Thy holy Name.[4]

That prayer would be answered abundantly. By April, however, Charles had received an offer of a curacy from his friend John Mayor, but there was no hesitation in declining the invitation:

I believe I must not entertain the thought of accepting it and leaving my present line of labouring in the Lord's vineyard. The fields here all over the country are white for the harvest. Fresh ground is daily gained … Thousands flock to hear and in many parts of the country … are effectually called … I cannot in conscience quit the field here … pray for me. I am often from the ground of my heart crying out, 'Who is sufficient for these things?'[5]

Weeks later as part of maintaining regular contact with his Anglican evangelical colleagues in England, he informed Edward Griffin:

I have good tidings to give you in general: The Lord has done great things in the face of all opposition and through weak means, within these forty years past, and his hand is stretched out still.[6]

---

4   DEJ, 1, 523-5

5   DEJ, 1, 539

6   Richard Bennett 'Llythurau y Parch. Thomas Charles', JHS, 5 (1920), pp. 41-2.

Instead of the spiritual darkness and immorality which prevailed over the previous decades, there were now prayer meetings, sermons, societies and associations attended by thousands. He thought there was gospel preaching often in most, if not all, parishes in both Anglesey and Caernarfonshire, while in Merioneth there remained several districts without preaching yet progress was being made '… and fresh places are continually opening.'

Societies

What about the Bala Society? In his letter to Edward Griffin (5 July 1785), Charles answered the question:

> At Bala there were but a half dozen hearers at the beginning, and the opposition continued without interruption for the space of 25 years. Now the congregation consists of about 2,000 hearers, and there are between 400 and 500 communicants … The Lord certainly has done a great work here: the preaching of the gospel has been attended, especially at seasons, with great visible power, and its effects … are evident to all…

How did Charles cope with the Bala situation alongside the demands of other areas in the North? He had two priorities. One priority was 'preaching the gospel in new places' and as a clergyman he was normally 'much more acceptable' to the people. His second priority was on Sundays to preach in different counties in North Wales where society members could attend and have the sacrament. He was only free, therefore, one Sunday a month to preach in Bala. No wonder he exclaimed: 'I have my hands full, as there is no clergyman but myself in the whole six counties. I am at times ready to sink under the burden…' so he begged for prayer support. Charles added: 'Our sacramental seasons are often very precious and we have much of the divine presence.'

What were these societies established by the Calvinistic Methodists?[7] They started in 1736, possibly earlier, as a result of Howell Harris' exhorting in caring for converts and those seeking the Lord. Early on, those attending were expected to be Anglicans as there was no desire to create a new denomination. The majority of members were ordinary and poor, including a significant number of young people. Three requirements were expected of prospective members: poverty of spirit, conviction of sin and a genuine desire to know and please God, yet the spiritual condition of those attending varied considerably. A 'steward' or 'exhorter' would care for one, two or three societies in his locality, while 'public exhorters' had oversight of about twelve societies with a superintendent responsible for the societies more widely.

Interestingly, Thomas Charles distinguished above and between *'communicants'* or members and *'hearers'*, a distinction which continued within the Presbyterian Church of Wales. Phenomenal growth was evident in the Bala Society with members and hearers attending from villages nearby and the powerful movement of the Holy Spirit upon the preaching continued to make these societies necessary. The 'one ruling desire and motive' within these societies, however, 'was a striving after God. They hungered and thirsted for his presence.'[8]

---

7 A readable and reliable account of these societies is provided by Emyr Roberts in *Revival in Wales: Addresses to the Bala Ministers' Conference*, edited by John Aaron and John Emyr (Bridgend: Bryntirion Press, 2014), pp. 71-90. This and other chapters in the book provide valuable information; both individuals and churches will find the contents challenging and useful.

8 *Revival in Wales*, p. 89

Schools

By March 1787, Charles was able to thank the Rev. Thomas Scott in England for money he raised to support the chapel in Dolgellau where there was considerable blessing and growth. He referred to the success of establishing charity schools to teach poor children and young people to read the Bible in their native language but also to 'teach them the principles of the Christian religion by catechising them'. The success was 'far beyond my expectations'. At this stage, seven schoolmasters were employed and paid £10 per annum; the teachers stayed in an area for between six to nine months before moving to another location. Money for their support was raised by Charles from clergy and friends in England then gradually from within societies, on a voluntary basis, in their desire to see the younger generation instructed in Christianity.

Charles carried an increasing burden in organising these schools in addition to preaching and caring for societies in North Wales. With regard to catechising children, Charles had made 'a short, clear, practical system of Divinity, with a text of Scripture annexed to every answer proving the doctrine advanced'. In addition, he added, 'I visit all the schools myself as often as I can.' By 1794, there were twenty teachers working in five counties in North Wales and Charles described the schools as 'little seminaries' where there was considerable blessing. In visiting each school and catechising the children publicly, the congregation would often be so large that it was necessary to hold the meeting in the open air. 'In some of the schools', he reports, 'we have had general awakenings among the young' making them attentive, biblically informed, providing a taster for reading and preparing them to attend preaching meetings. His main aim throughout this work was 'the salvation of souls' and the Lord was 'gloriously at work'.

Others had been involved in the education of children and young people before Charles. The Welsh Trust (1674–1681), the SPCK (1700–1727) and Griffith Jones (1734–1779) had all established charity schools with varying degrees of success. Charles admired the work of Griffith Jones and used that pattern by training teachers, using the Welsh language and the Bible; both men also wrote their own literature[9] for schools and used a catechism. Charles' schools, however, were more flexible, often placed in scattered communities apart from a parish church, although expecting local clergy support. His schools were not financed by the Church but by donations from societies, and outside donors. One fact stands out. The circulating schools became an important means by which Calvinistic Methodism thrived in Wales during this period.

Sunday schools

Initially Charles was not disposed to holding Sunday schools,[10] but again in God's providence this developed spontaneously out of the circulating schools work when some teachers introduced an additional lesson on Sunday evenings. Surprisingly, they found that more children, but especially adults who were free from work commitments, were eager to learn to read. For a number of years from 1787 this practice flourished but with a detrimental effect on

---

9 Charles' *Instructor* (*Hyfforddwr*) then at a later date his *Scriptural Dictionary* (*Geiriadur*), are examples.

10 While not the first person in England to begin a Sunday school, Robert Raikes (1735–1811) paid for four women in Gloucester to bring together boys and girls for the purpose of learning to read then recite the Catechism which led to a Sunday school movement throughout the country. Charles was aware of what Raikes was doing but it took time for him to accept then embrace the idea of a Sunday school not just for children but for all ages.

the circulating schools. What emerged was a powerful, extensive all-age Sunday school where children and adults in different groups were taught to read the Bible, receive instruction but also discuss and memorise the Scriptures. There was enormous spiritual benefit from this provision and by 1808 Charles arranged Sunday School Associations[11] where district Sunday schools united for a day's catechising of three or four hours in length. They were happy occasions with instruction given on practical subjects like parents/ children, husbands/wives, employers/employees and magistrates/ citizens. The Lord was at work.

In the next chapter we will look at Charles in the context of his own family in Bala.

---

11 They were known as Children's Associations.

8 Charles and Family

There was no hiding the pain and loss they both felt when Charles was away from home preaching. On such journeys, Charles expressed his feelings for Sally as the following letters indicate: 'I long to see you … with the greatest possible love…' (November 18, 1784); '… how can I be happy without you and at such a great distance?… You know I love you too dear to tell how much…' (May 1786); '…need I tell you that I love you? no: but still it is pleasing to me to repeat it, though you want no assurance of it. I bless the providence that brought us together. I do and shall love you…' (October 1787). Nor was Sally reticent in expressing her love for Charles: '…I think much of you – too much my dear dear C…' (November 1784), and she always felt 'much longing' for when her husband would return home (February1785). Her letter of June 1786 is another of many examples of her 'much longing to see you [Charles] once more at home'. Charles' itinerant preaching ministry in North Wales and beyond involving his care for the rapidly growing societies and schools was extremely demanding, requiring him to leave home regularly, sometimes for two or three weeks. The separation was difficult to bear.

Correspondence

Away from home, they corresponded regularly, sharing news and encouraging each other. Sally loved to share local and family news as well as referring to her spiritual needs. Charles' response was affectionate, supportive and pastoral in encouraging his wife. The question remains: how did Sally cope with regular, sometimes long periods of separation? And what about Charles?

Sally's earlier doubts about being the wife of an Anglican clergyman receded and she was encouraged that Charles now served amongst the Methodists rather than in a curacy. Several weeks after their marriage in the autumn of 1783, she expressed this encouragement in a letter to her beloved: '…I should be very unhappy on account of the long journeys if I did not think it answers a more glorious end than anything of a worldly nature, and I hope the Lord will honour you to be of use to his glory in the world.'[1] In view of the difficulties and opposition Charles had faced in his curacies from those who hated the gospel, Sally shared honestly in the same letter: 'I am glad my dear C is separated from amongst them; may Jesus the Captain of his host commission you to go out in the face of devils, the door is wide open to preach the gospel out of their synagogues…' The fact that this new ministry amongst Methodists had opened up for her husband and that he was the means of bringing many to faith and assurance became an important factor in Sally accepting enforced periods of separation. She could be content in the Lord's providence. That was her settled conviction though she could not hide the pain she felt when they were apart. Charles knew Sally was a 'praying wife' and her prayers meant a great deal to him, while Sally was comforted that Charles regularly supported her in prayer.

---

1   DEJ, 1, 446

Charles pastored his wife tenderly in his letters. Sally on one occasion referred in consecutive letters to her 'hard heart ... and stubbornness' but the presence of visitors and 'others interrupting all the time...' prevented her giving more detail, whereas in the next letter she confessed that 'my deadness under all the ordinances is a cause of grief to me. I am like one bound up in darkness and iron, I know not how nor which way to come out of my prison.' She desperately needed his prayers and wise counsel, so their times of prayer and sharing were a major encouragement to Sally in her struggles.

1785–1788

The year 1785 was significant for several reasons. Charles' close friend, John Lucas, in Somerset, died suddenly in his mid-forties. Describing Lucas as 'the dearest and most valuable friend I ever had', he added: 'Some of my happiest moments were spent in his company, and I received more instruction and benefit from him, than from all my other friends besides...'[2] Lucas had also supported him financially and Charles felt the bereavement deeply.

By contrast, nearly six months later, there was joy in the family when their first child, Thomas Rice Charles, was born, but by late October that year their joy was turned to sorrow when Sally's mother, Jane Foulkes, died. Over the years she had maintained a faithful and godly witness in the town during the long years of persecution as well as in the recent period of growth in the Bala Society. Charles had valued the love she and her husband extended to him, then the warm welcome into their home on marrying Sally. Charles helped in the family shop when Sally and her stepfather attended fairs in North Wales and Chester. Writing to Sally in early July 1786, he reported he

2 DEJ, 1, 532

had arrived home safely but 'much tired' due to Sunday preaching yet 'in good time' to help with the shop and look after their child, Thomas Rice. He also confessed to having 'many anxious thoughts about' Sally. Whether at home or on his travels, Charles and Sally were given grace to exercise a strong trust in the Lord in each situation. This is illustrated in a letter Charles wrote in comforting a lonely Christian in Somerset struggling with the mystery of providence. The words remain relevant:

> …you know he is all-sufficient. We can never trust too little in man, nor too much in God. I am convinced of this by daily experience. Our main point and study should be to keep close to God in daily communion; and he will take care of us and of all that belong to us. Has he given his Son to die for us; and will he not take care of us the few days we are on our journey to our Father's house? The thought is unworthy of him. No, my dear friend, we have not such a Father. Let us honour him and testify our good opinion of him by trusting him with the care of our souls and bodies – with our temporal and eternal concerns. Though all should forsake us and prove unfaithful, yet faith will say, 'This God is our God for ever and ever; and he will be our guide unto death.' Mark, he will be 'our guide unto death' – what can we want more this side of death? He is 'our God forever and ever' – here is enough after death and to all eternity. Here is a portion! Here is a husband! Here is a friend! Oh may we rejoice in him more and more! Can he be poor and friendless who has God for his God? Can his condition be bad who has all-sufficiency in possession? … we have a rich Father; and our elder Brother has all power and authority given him in heaven and earth … look upon the riches, the glory, the peace and the joy which are at the Lord's right hand. 'Lord, 'tis enough that thou art mine.'

From these words, we see further Charles' biblical view of the Lord's providence which was not mere mental assent to doctrine. Even in periods of stress, sadness, separation and bereavement, they endeavoured to trust the Lord, whatever happened, good or bad.

For example, their second child Sarah was born in February 1787, but Sally was extremely ill for three weeks before delivering the child. Charles 'was obliged to live above a week (and a most trying week it was) tossed between hope and fear … the whole of her recovery is the Lord's doing, and I believe in answer to prayer in extremity. It is well to have an all-sufficient Friend to go to. When I gave her up to him, I received her back from him… We cannot but see the Lord's hand in it from first to last…'[3]

Their faith was frequently tested. In May 1787, Charles' father died at his home, Cil-y-coed, a farm near Meidrim, Carmarthen. There were legal and financial difficulties involved with his estate which Charles and the family found demanding. In October that same year while preaching in South Wales, Sally informed Charles that a fire had broken out in the kitchen chimney and the 'flames were so furious'. Sally, 'immediately alarmed with fear', especially fearing that one of the children would be hurt, reported that no one was injured and she was amazed to find 'everything just as it was before'. Sally recognised the Lord's providence with the fire occurring during the day rather than at night when they were sleeping; 'It is the arm of the Lord and I know it calls for our humiliation and praises.'[4]

In November that year, a huge shock awaited Sally and Charles. Sally's stepfather, Thomas Foulkes, informed them he was going to remarry; to marry Sally's closest friend and peer, Lydia Lloyd, with whom Sally had shared deeply for years. Lydia was twenty-six

3 DEJ, 1, 568-9

4 DEJ, 1, 585-6

years younger than Sally's stepfather. Although Sally was now the sole owner of the shop, she had valued the help of her stepfather, especially in accompanying her to fairs. In respect for Sally and on Charles' advice, he relocated to Machynlleth to open a shop there with his new bride, rather than compete in business in Bala.

Faith was severely tested again within weeks, for in January 1788, Sally and Charles' daughter Sarah died just before her first birthday after months of 'almost continual affliction and sorrow'. Once again, they were enabled to face the bereavement in faith and submission to the Lord. That same year, his favourite sister Elizabeth lost her husband, and then by May 1789 Elizabeth herself died leaving four orphaned children. While studying in Carmarthen, Charles had stayed with this family for six years and was deeply attached to them, so their four-year-old son David was fostered by them in Bala; however he died at the age of fourteen.

On their tenth wedding anniversary in August 1793, Charles was in London for eight weeks preaching at Lady Huntingdon's chapel at Spa Fields. In his letter to Sally marking their anniversary, Charles wrote:

> During that time the Lord has made you the means of great comfort to me. He gave me the only person I desired and hath blessed our connection. Though we have not been without trials, yet we have not had them from each other. No person in the world is happier in this respect than myself. I would not change my position for the Imperial crown…[5]

His last preaching commitment was on Sunday evening, 8 September after which he was free to return home. Many appreciated his preaching but importantly there were opportunities to meet

5   DEJ, 11, 123-4

supportive evangelical clergymen and laypeople who would prove valuable contacts as his ministry developed. Clearly his London visits were vital in gaining practical and prayerful support for the work in Wales. The fee paid to him for preaching was used to complete the purchase of a house in Bala. While Charles was away, Sally had been busy caring for their home, organising the shop and looking after their son. Sally was a hard worker, skilled in business, persevering, kind yet firm in supervising the servants who undertook housework and assisted in the shop.[6] Affectionate by nature, Sally was widely respected in the area. Following her mother's death, Sally had sole responsibility for the shop and providentially her income was able to support her family and Charles' ministry after their marriage until 1810. This was the Lord's provision.

In the next chapter we will learn of the remarkable growth which took place in the work of the gospel.

---

6   Gwen Emyr *Sally Jones: Rhodd Duw i Charles,* (Pen-y-bont ar Ogwr, Gwasg Efengylaidd Cymru, 1996), p. 17.

9 Remarkable Growth

It was July 1795. Charles had just returned from attending his mother's funeral in South Wales and was delighted to be home again in Bala. However, within a few days he needed to travel to London for eight weeks of preaching in Spa Fields, visits which were important for the work in Wales and more widely. There were considerable pressures on Charles in leading the Calvinistic Methodists in North and South Wales following the deaths of Daniel Rowland (1791) and another influential leader, William Williams, Pantycelyn, who also died in 1791. Both men were sorely missed and only a few days before he died, Williams had written to Charles seeking more of Charles' ministry:

> …A visit from some of your preachers is much needed in south Wales. Of the preachers owned of God, six or seven are either dead or afflicted of the Lord, and the north Wales preachers most in favour with the people have not visited us for some time. You yourself are one of them, because your services are called for from every part of south Wales, and the Lord will reward you if you come… A great

revival has taken place in many parts of our country… Welsh schools are much needed in order to teach the Word of God…[1]

Dolgellau

One of the areas affected by revival which Williams knew about was Dolgellau, a town nestling in the foothills of Cader Idris and lying on the River Wnion, a tributary of the River Mawddach. Charles was very familiar with the town and referring in 1787 to a new Methodist chapel built there, he reported that despite 'the mountainous country surrounding that little town, the gospel spreads powerfully'. What happened? Many who had never heard the gospel were converted and the change in many lives was 'wonderful to see'. Charles described it as 'the outpouring of the Spirit', a work which 'still continues at times so abundant and powerful among those who made the utmost opposition to it…' The impact on people in the area was extensive and powerful.

Bala

Charles also referred to a similar powerful working of God's Spirit in Bala in 1791. This revival was unexpected. Charles explained he was preaching in Bala twice that Sunday with the afternoon service being 'no more' than what he usually experienced amongst believers there. A remarkable difference however, occurred towards the close of the evening service when a great number of people who had never sought God before began to cry out, 'What must I do to be saved' and, 'God be merciful to me a sinner.' By late evening, only 'cries and groans of people in distress of soul' could be heard throughout the town. Deep conviction of sin gripped the entire congregation and

---

1   DEJ, 1, 11, 51-5

those living in the area. People of all ages were affected yet mostly young people. Prayer meetings were held during the following days and only eternal concerns occupied people's minds. Conviction of sin 'spread so rapidly' that 'there was hardly a young person in the neighbourhood' unaffected. Several other features of this revival are worth mentioning. It continued 'with unabated power and glory, spreading from one town to another, all around this part of the country'. Charles had never seen or expected such a glorious work and 'would not have been without seeing what I now see in the land. – No, not for the world'. He shared that 'it is an easy and delightful work to preach the glorious gospel … for many are the fervent prayers put up by the people for the preacher' so that 'beams of divine light, together with irresistible energy, accompany every truth delivered…'

Writing to a friend about the Bala revival he explains: 'I can hardly believe my eyes sometimes when I see in our chapels those who were the most faithful servants of Satan, weeping, in the greatest distress, under a sense of sin and danger and crying out for mercy…'[2] Charles helpfully describes this revival in six ways as: '1. *A very gracious work*; grace abounds towards the chief of sinners. 2. *A very powerful work;* convictions are deep and overpowering. 3. It's a *short work;* there is little preparative work. 4. *It is a growing work,* not only because it spreads wider and wider in the country … but it grows and thrives in the souls of those where it is begun… 5. It is a pretty *general* work also in terms of people dealt with. 6. A *lasting* work'.

A lot happened for Charles between 1790 and July 1795 before he left for another London preaching visit. For example, in 1790 Charles was asked to provide *Rules for the Proper Order and Propriety*

---

2   DEJ, 11, 89-95

in the Associations or Quarterly Meetings and in this and other related ways his gifts and leadership were recognised. Opposition to gospel preaching continued, as Charles found when preaching in the open air in Corwen in 1790. Those living there were opposed to Methodist activity or presence so, unsurprisingly, when Charles began preaching the local blacksmith signalled the locals quickly by beating a drum. They promptly arrived, throwing stones at the preacher, one achieving a direct hit on his mouth, so he had to leave.

Excommunication

There was also a complex matter concerning the excommunication of a well-known leader of the Methodist movement, Peter Williams (1723–1813) from the Carmarthen area. He was a curate in the Anglican Church but had not been ordained as a priest due to his Methodist views so in 1747 he joined the Methodist Society in Newcastle Emlyn. He became an itinerant Methodist preacher for over forty years, during which time he suffered considerable persecution and cruelty in the cause of the gospel. Williams was well known because of his itinerant ministry as well as his sacrificial service for the Lord so that Christians respected him greatly.

Williams' popularity increased when in 1770 he published an edition of the Welsh Bible, including his notes on each chapter. This edition of the Bible became extremely popular and was reprinted many times, but to help poorer people obtain a cheaper edition, he translated and published an English edition of the Bible in 1790, but again with his own notes, even changing some Bible texts like Proverbs 8:25, Matthew 1:20 and Luke 1:35. There had been concerns expressed regarding the 1770 Bible edition, particularly his notes on Proverbs 8:25 and John chapter 1 which suggested the Lord Jesus was not a distinct Person from the Father. His heresy became much clearer in the 1790 edition where, for example, in Luke 1:35 he changed the Bible text from 'that *holy one*' to 'that *holy thing*', adding: 'the *Man* Jesus is not a *different person* from the Father…' Increasing concern was expressed over Williams' view of the Trinity in the 1770 edition, but strong support for Williams continued because of his valiant efforts for the gospel over the years. His 1790 Bible edition, especially his accompanying notes, was recognised by many as undermining the doctrine of the Holy Trinity – Father, Son and Holy Spirit. The situation was even more serious.

Before his death in 1791, William Williams, Pantycelyn, wrote several letters to Charles, sharing his concerns for the work. His penultimate letter in May 1790 shared concerns over errors creeping into the movement relating to the Trinity. Referring to 'Articles of the Church in England, the Nicene and Athanasian Creeds, the lesser and larger Catechisms of the Assembly with their Confession of Faith', he reminded Charles that, 'our young exhorters should study such orthodox tracts over and over again.' That need Charles met in writing resources for leaders and believers but more of that later. The South Wales Association of Methodists in their two meetings in 1791 decided to excommunicate Peter Williams from their movement which was confirmed by the North Wales Association. Williams was forbidden to visit and teach in their societies or sell his Bible.

When Peter Williams died, Charles graciously acknowledged his faithful, sacrificial work for the gospel over many years: 'He was the means of conferring great blessings on many souls in the dark days in which he lived… Some of his remarks on the doctrine of the Trinity gave offence to many, and stirred up strife and controversies… This Bible (1770) was a precious gift to monoglot Welshmen' but due to the alterations he made to the text of the 1790 edition of the Bible with the accompanying comments, the Methodist movement was unable to commend it yet, 'respect for him was not diminished in the eyes of many.'[3]

For Charles, Williams was a brother in the Lord rather than an enemy, yet he strayed from the precious doctrine of the Person of Christ, a doctrine which requires upholding, however faithful or popular the proponent of a heresy may be. Charles' involvement in this excommunication would have been extensive. Peter Williams himself recognised this fact, informing his son in May 1791: 'I am told that Charles of Bala is determined ... to expel me from this Connexion entirely...' Charles may have been too involved in this process of excommunication, but again sound doctrine was important for him and the work.

'A high privilege'

There were many essential matters for Charles to deal with. He was continually visiting and establishing circulating schools, ministering the Word in societies as well as raising money for his schools, Sunday schools and for building Methodist chapels, as in Liverpool (1787). He was also a trustee for some societies and chapels in North Wales, so the demands on him were considerable.

No wonder before leaving for London in July 1795, he wrote to a friend explaining his circumstances:

I have nearly dropped all my correspondents ... both my time and thoughts are much occupied ... a large family, the extensive business in which my wife is engaged and besides, I may add without boasting, 'the care of all the churches' in these parts... But I have been by Providence brought into it without any design of my own; and now... every other consideration must give way to the

---

3 *Trysorfa Ysbrydol* (1813), 483-5; DEJ, 11, 281-2.

faithful discharge of the trust committed to me… I desire to labour, that I may be accepted of Him… Not only have I my own concerns, but also everybody's burdens; and everyone's trials must be mine also: but I do not complain. I see it as an honour and a high privilege to be thus employed by my Divine Master…[4]

Like previous visits to London, it was a busy but profitable eight weeks for Charles. His preaching engagements on Sundays while in London were in the Countess of Huntingdon's chapel at Spa Fields. The Countess was a good friend and supporter of Charles in his ministry in Wales but died in April 1791. However, this support continued as the four trustees appreciated his ministry and his labours for the Lord.

Overseas mission

Charles' three years in Oxford, followed by curacies in England, had introduced him to the wider gospel work and to leaders who would support his work. Charles' interests were not confined to Wales. In 1792, for example, he had met with an exhorter in the Methodist Society in Waunfawr, Caernarfonshire, John Evans, who sailed that year for America to evangelise the Indians and a lost Welsh tribe! Evans met with little success. In 1792, the Baptist Missionary Society was formed under the influence of William Carey; three years later some evangelical Anglicans, Presbyterians, Calvinistic Methodists and Independents agreed to establish the London Missionary Society (LMS). Charles became one of its mission directors, committed to prayer and support for worldwide mission. A year later in 1796 thirty missionaries sailed for the South Sea Islands but beforehand Charles dined aboard the ship with the captain. Months later, he

---

4 DEJ, 11, 154

wrote down his impressions of that occasion and the thrill of seeing the missionaries setting sail:

> I felt great joy and thankfulness on the occasion. While I could see … many hundreds of vessels trading to different parts of the globe, engaged in conveying the perishable treasures of this world from one nation to another. I could see ONE … trading for heaven, the great cause of the gospel, and the salvation of immortal souls…[5]

Charles then described meetings with the LMS directors and their examination of candidates as missionaries. His response?

> …I felt proud of them … spiritual men … and devoted to the work. There is need of still more missionaries and … money … and prayers of all on behalf of this most important task.

But there was need of more people: 'godly, spiritual men, enlightened by the gospel', whatever their skills.

For Charles, zeal was grounded in biblical, theological motivation for missionary work. He wondered whether 'the secret wheels of Providence are hasting the fulfilment of the prophecies' of the Old Testament, 'glorious tasks' involving 'the destruction of Antichrist, the calling of the Gentiles, the conversion of the Jews. Then the kingdoms of this world shall become the kingdoms of the Lord and of his Christ; and he shall reign forever and forever… Rev. 19:6' He added importantly: 'It has been, on many occasions, no small comfort to my weak mind, to be able to believe, on the basis of the Scriptures, that we labour in a work that is *certain of success*.' Charles did not major on aspects of eschatology but, influenced by Jonathan Edwards in America, William Williams, Pantycelyn, Thomas Boston in Scotland and others, he expected a period prior to the return of

---

5 DEJ, 11, 188-190

the Lord Jesus Christ in glory when the preaching of the gospel of Christ would enjoy 'great success' worldwide involving the salvation of many Jews and Gentiles. Charles would have heartily endorsed the words of the hymn written by William Williams, Pantycelyn:

> O'er the gloomy hills of darkness,
> Look, my soul, be still, and gaze,
> All the promises do travail
> With a glorious day of Grace:
> Blessed jubilee!
> Let thy glorious morning dawn.
>
> Kingdoms wide that sit in darkness,
> Grant them, Lord, Thy glorious light;
> And from eastern coast to western
> May the morning chase the night;
> And redemption,
> Freely purchased, win the day.
>
> May the glorious day approaching
> End their night of sin and shame,
> And the everlasting gospel
> Spread abroad Thy holy Name
> O'er the borders
> Of the great Immanuel's land.
>
> Fly abroad, thou mighty gospel,
> Win and conquer, never cease;
> May thy lasting wide dominion
> Multiply and still increase!
> Sway Thy sceptre,
> Saviour, all the world around.

But whether in Wales or overseas, more and more Bibles were needed for people to read in their own languages. That is the theme of the next chapter.

10 Bibles – More Needed!

Welsh language Bibles were scarce during the eighteenth century. And if available at all they were expensive. There was also the problem that many people were unable to read or write. The Welsh Trust in the previous century, established by Thomas Gouge (1605(?)–1681), a London philanthropist, had aimed to instruct children to read and learn about the Christian faith, but this was mostly done in English rather than in the native Welsh language. Following Gouge's death and that of his fellow Puritans, Stephen Hughes and Charles Edwards, their work of publishing and teaching was continued by the Anglican-sponsored SPCK[1] with Sir John Philipps as its leader in Wales. The SPCK established 120 Charity Schools for children in Wales and printed some Welsh Bibles and other books. When the Rev. Griffith Jones married Sir John's sister, his own circulating schools developed and expanded this earlier work. By 1731, four years prior to the outbreak of the Methodist revival, Jones's circulating schools had begun and increased to 220 before he died.[2] Charles' circulating

---

1 Society for the Propagation of Christian Knowledge.

2 A helpful resource is *The Christian Heritage of Welsh Education,* R. M. Jones and Gwyn Davies, Bryntirion Press/Association of Christian Teachers of Wales,

schools built on this background but they were also different, before becoming 'the principal means of erecting Sunday Schools',[3] which became influential throughout Wales, catering for all ages. Due to the scarcity of Bibles, Charles' aims in the Sunday schools included teaching scholars to read, but also to memorise chapters of the Bible and understand Bible teaching. He refers, for example, to a five-year-old girl 'who can repeat distinctly above a hundred chapters out, and goes on learning a chapter every week, besides learning the catechism, and searching the Scriptures for passages on different points in divinity...'[4] But there was an urgent need for more Welsh Bibles and especially as, in addition, 'thousands are perishing for lack of knowledge.'

Mary Jones

Mary Jones was a fifteen-year-old who in 1800 walked twenty-six miles alone and barefoot over the mountains from Llanfihangel-y-Pennant, near Towyn to Bala. Her purpose was to purchase a Welsh Bible.

Mary's background is interesting. Her family was poor; her father, a weaver, had died when she was very young. At the age of eight, accompanying her widowed mother regularly to the local society meeting, she came to personal faith in the Lord Jesus and gained a good understanding of the Bible. She longed to read the Bible herself, but there were only two copies of the Bible in her area. One was in the parish church and the other in a farmhouse two miles from her home. After receiving permission from the farmer's wife,

---

1986.

3 Letter of Thomas Charles, January 4th, 1811.

4 Letter of Thomas Charles to Alderman Lea in London who was a generous supporter of the Sunday School Society and the Bible Society; 1808.

Mary walked to the farmhouse weekly in all kinds of weather for a period of six years to read the Bible, memorising as many verses as possible. Mary saved all the money she earned from helping neighbours until eventually she had enough money to buy a Bible. Professor Wyn James reminds us:

> For someone as poor as Mary Jones, saving enough money to buy a Bible was a great sacrifice. Bibles were very expensive … and she would have had to have scrimped and saved every penny for years before succeeding to accumulate the little over seventeen shillings she would have needed to buy a Bible – a huge sum for a poor girl like Mary.[5]

Mary Jones walked to Bala for a Bible because Thomas Charles lived there and was known to be making valiant efforts to obtain Welsh Bibles for the people. As early as 1787, Charles had been deeply concerned to obtain cheap copies of the Welsh Bible. As the schools and Sunday schools' work gathered momentum, Bibles were desperately needed as increasing numbers of people longed to read and possess the Bible. The revivals occurring in the last twenty-five years of the eighteenth century with thousands of new converts, added urgency to the need for Bibles.

Charles, actively seeking to obtain Welsh Bibles from England, felt frustrated by the slow response of those who could have helped. His concern was expressed in a letter (17 March 1787) to his friend, Rev. Thomas Scott:

> You ask me 'whether a parcel of Welsh Bibles would be acceptable?' You could think of nothing more acceptable, more wanted and useful to the country at large. I have been often, in my journeys

---

5 Professor E. Wyn James, www.anngriffiths.cardiff.ac/Bible.html suggests the sum involved was 3s.6d; DEJ, 11, 492-4, 519.

through different parts of the country at large, questioned, whether I knew where a Welsh Bible could be bought for a small price. And it has hurt my mind much to be obliged to answer in the negative. There are none to be bought for money, unless some poor person pinched by poverty is obliged to sell his Bible to support himself and family … I think I could … make profitable use of any quantity you could procure for me…[6]

Scott succeeded in sending Charles a small supply of Bibles while other friends like John Thornton obtained 100 copies for Charles from SPCK, then his son Henry Thornton with William Wilberforce persuaded SPCK to print a larger number of Welsh Bibles.

It was during this period that Mary Jones arrived in Bala to purchase a copy of the Welsh Bible. Arriving at Charles' home, she was told he had no Bibles because further supplies had not yet arrived. The exact details of what happened are uncertain. One close friend of Mary Jones was Lizzie Rowlands who visited Mary several times a week when she was old. Written seventy years after the event, Lizzie recalled what Mary herself had shared with her. On reaching Bala and requesting a Bible from Charles, she was told he was expecting more Bibles, so he arranged for her to stay with a former servant until they arrived. There is no indication how long she waited but when the Bibles arrived, Lizzie recalls Mary saying that Charles gave her three Bibles for the price of one. The details are uncertain but probably she received the 1799 SPCK edition of the Bible.

Bible Society

Many more Welsh Bibles were needed. Could one society be given the task of producing Welsh Bibles? Charles was preaching in Spa

---

6 DEJ, 1, 566-7

Fields so was able to attend a meeting of the Religious Tract Society (RTS) in London in autumn, 1802. After the meeting he shared with a member his burden that many more copies of the Welsh Bible were urgently required. That member was Joseph Tarn from Spa Fields Chapel who was Charles' close friend. Tarn was moved deeply by what Charles told him. At the next RTS committee meeting in November when Charles was absent, Tarn shared about the desperate need for Welsh Bibles and the concern Charles felt. They invited Charles to address the next RTS committee in December to hear more about the need in Wales. The day before the December meeting, Charles realised that a separate society was required which only produced Welsh Bibles. His suggestion was welcomed and a decision was made to publicise the need, but extended later to Bibles in 'various languages', not just Welsh. The following months were characterised by weekly RTS meetings in London with sensitivity needed to avoid giving any impression of competing with SPCK. Eventually, with leaders like William Wilberforce and others giving support, the new society was named as 'The British and Foreign Bible Society' (BFBS) and was launched on the 7th March 1804 with the exclusive task of printing Bibles in different languages for 'gratuitous distribution' – a fact which avoided rivalry with SPCK.

The story of Mary Jones[7] and her sacrificial efforts to obtain a copy of the Bible in Wales had influenced those in London who

---

7 There is an attractive Mary Jones World site on the edge of Bala in Llanycil Church. 'Mary Jones World is an award-winning state-of-the-art visitor and education centre that tells the story of Mary Jones and Thomas Charles, and the impact of the world's bestselling book – on Wales and the world. Step back in time, follow Mary's journey, and explore what happened next through multimedia and interactive displays, exhibits and activities in this redeveloped Grade 2-listed building. See Thomas Charles' inkwell and pay a visit to his grave. Set on the edge of Llyn Tegid (Bale Lake), with an on-site cafe, picnic area, facilities and children's playground, Mary Jones World offers a great time out for children and adults alike.'

heard of the need for Welsh Bibles from Charles, yet Mary was only one of many who longed to possess a Bible. A considerable amount of work was left in the capable hands of Charles with regard to the accuracy of the Bible text although he was assisted by others like Thomas Jones, Denbigh. Charles spent as many as ten hours most days in his study with the help of two assistants on this task as he pored over the Hebrew and Greek text as well as comparing other translations.

Excitement

Despite frustrations, the first delivery of 500 New Testaments reached Bala on the 25th September 1806. There was excitement in Bala as the carrier of the Testaments with his horse and cart approached with crowds of people flocking to escort him and his precious cargo into town. Entering Bala, crowds of people blocked the streets as people tried to snatch a copy of the New Testament. The 500 copies were sold immediately, and a further order was placed for another 913 copies, including 500 for Charles, with the rest ordered by shopkeepers in the area. A year later the Bibles arrived at Bala, but Charles was disappointed as there were flaws in it which needed rectifying. Charles' intensive work preparing for this edition of the Bible – which he had insisted must not include notes on the biblical text – had been considerable as well as exhausting. His expertise was further required by the SPCK for their new edition, called the '1809 Bible', in correcting the proofs. He was also tasked with editing and preparing the 1814 BFBS Welsh Bible which became popular due to its larger type but also for the accurate editing undertaken by Charles. This became the standard text for future editions printed by both SPCK and the BFBS. Charles' expertise as a result of ten years of working on the biblical text bore fruit in this 1814 edition of the

Bible. In 1809, the BFBS Committee elected Charles an Honorary Life Governor to acknowledge his outstanding work done on their behalf.

Fundraising

Who would pay for the costs of producing Bibles in Welsh and other languages? Charles did not shirk from his responsibility and he became an outstanding advocate for the BFBS. In addition to raising money for Sunday schools, the building of chapels, and the London Missionary Society, he successfully raised monies for the Bible Society. The latter involved Charles in additional administrative work like correspondence and keeping accounts but this was a delight for him. One letter (18 January 1805) reveals the way he approached the fundraising and how humbled he felt in witnessing the sacrificial giving of poor believers:

> I printed a small pamphlet in the Welsh language, containing principally, accounts of Missions, and their various success in several parts of the world … with a view of exciting a missionary spirit among our people … [who] had no conception that a large proportion of mankind are destitute of the word of God… After my pamphlet was pretty generally dispersed, and I had talked it over with different persons of all persuasions, of any influence in the country, I began my work… I introduced … the formation of the new Bible Society, the necessity of it… Soon after this little publication was dispersed and read pretty generally, I was frequently accosted by one and another of our pious people, expressing their joy that such a Society was formed, and their hopes that public collections would be made in our congregations towards the support of so glorious a work.

Charles began collecting for this work in August 1804. Explaining that his congregations were poor, though numerous with hundreds, sometimes thousands, of people attending, he was overwhelmed by the sacrificial giving of many poor people in their meetings. Charles felt inadequate describing how he felt seeing poor people giving sacrificially to the work of providing Bibles in different languages. He continued his letter:

> When I informed them of the countless millions in the world, of guilty and miserable sinners like themselves, who had no Bibles, were without Christ, and without God in the world, but were worshipping stones, logs of wood, beasts, etc. and plunging themselves into rivers, to cleanse themselves from their sins, totally ignorant of the fountain opened for sins and uncleanness, I saw hundreds bathed in tears, and overwhelmed with sorrow and compassion.

Charles' appeal for financial support was not based on emotion but on the prophecies and promises of Scripture which encouraged the congregations. Referring to his experience of standing at the door after speaking, he referred to the joy of these poor folk 'dropping their mites in the plate; especially young persons … mothers … a father with his ten children together, each dropping a small piece of money in the plate.' He mentioned these examples to highlight God's grace evident in their sacrificial giving but also their love of God's Word and 'the hearty prayers of thousands of them daily' for the Society's success in the world.[8]

'A friend to all'

That is how Charles described the Bible on one occasion: 'The Bible is a friend to all who love him, and can give them consolations, strong, divine and eternal.'[9] He continued:

8 DEJ, 11, 551-3.

9 John Aaron *The Life of Thomas Charles of Bala (1755–1814),* (unpublished, 2018), p. 269.

You can never change him for a better friend; he is a tried one. You can converse with him at any hour of the day or night, silently and privately. And his advice is that of the highest wisdom and goodness, and may be safely relied on and followed... On the bed of languishing, there is no such sympathising and supporting friend to be found for love or money ... he will accompany you through death, as far as you need him, and will point out a brighter world before you, as an everlasting inheritance; where you will want him no more, but shall certainly enjoy all the rich promises therein made to you.

Writing in his *Geiriadur*, Charles outlines a clear doctrine of Scripture concerning its divine inspiration and origin, perfection, sufficiency and necessity:

The Holy Scriptures are a treasury of all profitable and necessary information. As they have all been given by the inspiration of God they must partake of His perfection and be worthy of him ... they cannot fail... He would not deceive us in anything ... the knowledge given to us in the Scriptures is supreme, certain and complete. There is nothing relating to our situation and happiness in another world, nor anything relating to our circumstances and duties here ... that God has not provided complete guidance for us in his Holy Word as to our behaviour in everything... The glorious plan of salvation by means of a Mediator shines clearly and fully in them before a world of sinners.

Here are solid reasons why he treasured the Bible and laboured to provide Bibles, and as accurate a Bible text as possible, for Wales and overseas.

His varied ministry with his passion to obtain more and more Bibles for Wales and the world was demanding as well as exhausting and this will be illustrated in the next chapter.

11 Demands of Ministry

In September 1799, Charles returned to Bala after his weeks of preaching in London, with frequent committee meetings[1] and appointments with important individuals; the Welsh Calvinistic Methodist Society in London also required his help. Exhausted, he was thrilled to be with his family once again. His son Thomas Rice and adopted nephew David Thomas were both fourteen years old and were being educated in Shrewsbury.

Frostbitten

There were many invitations for him to preach and visit the growing number of societies and Sunday schools. His preaching was valued, with some sermons being blessed to melt and stir congregations, like the sermon delivered in the Bontuchel Association near Ruthin in December 1785, when the people never forgot his message from Galatians 4:4. He was in demand. In December 1799 while on a preaching tour in the North, Charles received an urgent message that

---

1 His first appointments to directorships were in 1797 (London Missionary Society) and 1798 (Sunday Schools Society). Annual Board meetings of these societies were held during his prolonged visits to London.

his nephew was seriously ill and had been sent home from school to Bala with his son. Despite bitterly cold weather, he rode home to Bala through mountainous terrain but his left thumb became frostbitten through holding the horse's reins. Sadly, his nephew David died. Charles explained: '…it is our great joy and comfort … he knew Jesus as the Saviour and friend of sinners, and looked to him solely as the refuge and sole hope for salvation.'

Due to frostbite, Charles' hand became infected and extremely painful. For months he was often unable to work, sometimes Sally writing down what he dictated. Medical doctors recommended the amputation of his thumb while Christians in Bala and throughout Wales prayed for Charles' recovery. On the eve of the amputation in Chester, a prayer meeting was held in Charles' home. The highlight was Richard Owen, the local shoemaker and deacon in the Bala Society, who prayed earnestly and believingly for Charles' recovery based on the promise made to King Hezekiah (2 Kings 20:6: '…I will add to your days fifteen years…'). He repeated the request several times with conviction and assurance until all knew the prayer was answered. Charles lived for almost fifteen years afterwards!

'An amazing sight'

During his illness and months of recovery, he knew the Lord's presence in powerful ways with 'daily proofs of the Lord's great faithfulness in fulfilling his promises graciously made to us in his word.'[2] On recognising his serious physical condition, the Lord had

---

2 Robert Roberts, Clynnog, a powerful preacher, received a letter from Sally reporting her husband's ill-health. Roberts replied to Sally and Charles on 14 February 1801 apologising for his inabilty to visit them in their trial while also expressing his concern for the spiritual condition of Wales. See Llythyr v11:'Robert Roberts at Thomas Charles o'r Bala' 14 February 1801 in *Robert Roberts: Yr Angel o Glynnog,* Emyr Roberts & E.Wyn James (Llyfrgell Efengylaidd Cymru: Pen-y-bont ar Ogwr, 1976), No.3, pp. 45-7, 54-5.

given him 'such glorious views of Himself as produced a comfortable, calm frame of mind and *joyful* resignation to his will'. He claims:

> During the whole of my disposition I had daily proofs of the Lord's great faithfulness in fulfilling his promises graciously made to us in the word. As my day of trial or suffering was, so was my strength. Soon after the commencement of my complaint, when I understood the very serious consequences likely to follow, he graciously favoured me with such glorious views of HIMSELF as produced a comfortable, calm frame of mind and joyful resignation to his will. I never had such views before (…in the same degree of clearness and continuance) of his sovereignty, and justice … goodness and tenderness … It was an amazing sight, by faith, of a crucified Saviour, that conquered all the rebellions of my will, and banished all my fears. Under whatever character I viewed the Lord, I could not help loving him, and having confidence in him, and rejoicing with joy unspeakable and full of glory.[3]

The Lord he trusted and preached was gloriously real to him.

Preaching

Following his illness, Charles was in considerable demand. He continued preaching in Wales and further afield, including places like Liverpool, Manchester, Shropshire, London and even Ireland. Congregations were numerous, wherever he went. In Liverpool 'thousands attended every time'. In Wrexham he preached outside in English to over a thousand people whose attention was riveted on the gospel message.

Early in 1803, his itinerant ministry had to be postponed briefly. Providentially, he was at home in Bala when a messenger informed

---

3 DEJ, 11, 338-9.

him that his wife and son had met with an accident outside the town. They were travelling in a gig when one wheel passed over a heap of mud on the road which had the effect of lowering one side of the gig and throwing Thomas Rice on to the floor. He broke his leg, the frightened horse bolted and one wheel crashed into stones forming part of a small bridge. Sally was thrown to the ground, bruised and in pain. A medical doctor accompanied Charles to the scene and for weeks mother and son were nursed at home. Charles' care for his wife impressed people in the area. He remained at her bedside continually, washing her bruises and applying lotions provided by the doctor. Locals respected the way this preacher loved and cared for his wife and son.

There were occasions when Charles declined invitations to preach. For example, when the LMS invited him to preach at their Annual Meeting in London in May 1806, he declined but he was pressed to reconsider because of the meeting's importance. He finally accepted the invitation but also agreed to a three-week tour of North and mid-Wales with his friend, Rev. Rowland Hill (1744–1833) in the same period. Hill, although ordained as a curate, had been refused ordination by the bishops, so he became a popular English preacher and pastor of Surrey Independent Chapel in London. Like Charles, Hill was heavily involved in supporting the Bible Society and the London Missionary Society while also serving as chairman of the Religious Tract Society. They would have known and respected each other, so this tour in Wales was important for both men and the churches they visited.

Again in 1807, Charles was busy: '…all over the country, the schools prosper more than ever… I have catechised hundreds of children before thousands of people, once, twice, or three times, besides preaching … no uncommon thing with us for whole families

… to learn the catechisms and chapters, and to come and repeat them together.'

Associations

Other demands for preaching and help related to association meetings were necessary as well as preaching occasions for the public, with opportunities for preachers and exhorters to discuss matters relating to their societies and chapels. Monthly local meetings for preachers and exhorters were represented in the associations held quarterly. From the 1790s one annual association would be in Bala and one annual Southern association in Llangeitho. In the 1767 association in Bala only 200 people attended, but numbers increased. When John Elias started preaching in the Bala association from 1797, large crowds attended. In the Bala association of 1807, John Elias preached powerfully in the enlarged chapel building from Ephesians 3:17-19 with an 'enormous crowd' outside listening and a 'large congregation packed into the chapel'. Describing the amazing love of God early in the sermon, Elias rebuked some for shouting and rejoicing as they were preventing those who had travelled a distance from hearing the message. Tears galore were shed under the sound of the gospel, but so powerful was the preaching that afterwards many people were unable to restrain themselves in praising the Lord.

Writing

The catechisms[4] had been written by Charles to teach the Bible so all would remember. Charles needed to write such resources because

---

4 *A Summary of the Principles of Religion:* or a *Short Catechism to be learnt by children and others*: 1789; also, *An Evangelical Catechism*, 1797; although having the same title, Charles wrote in 1799 a different *Summary of the Principles of religion*: or a *Short Catechism for children and others, to learn.* By 1808 a 6th edition of this work had been published.

of the heretical teaching of Peter Williams' Bible notes concerning Christ's deity and then Arminian teaching reaching North Wales from 1800 with the Wesleyan Methodists. Truth was important even when Sally's stepfather, Thomas Foulkes, began openly espousing Arminian theology from his home in Machynlleth.[5]

In 1799 Charles co-edited *Trysorfa Ysbrydol* (A Spiritual Treasury) with Thomas Jones (1756–1820), Denbigh, who became the senior theologian for the Welsh Calvinistic Methodists and Charles' close friend. This helped to satisfy the hunger of thousands of converts in Wales and was the first periodical of its kind; included in it was news of the Lord's work in Wales and overseas, historical articles, minutes of Methodist associations, a sermon, doctrinal teaching as well as a poetry section. The 'Connexion' – a term referring to the Calvinistic Methodist movement and its churches – adopted the periodical but only six issues were produced due to illness and it was Charles who relaunched it later under the title of *Trysorfa* (Treasury).[6]

Geiriadur (Dictionary)

Charles also wrote *An Exposition of the Ten Commandments*[7] and began the massive task of writing a *Scriptural Dictionary* (*Geiriadur Ysgrythurol*) in four volumes published respectively in 1805, 1808, 1810 and 1811. A further six editions of his *Geiriadur* were published prior to 1900 and two editions in the United States. In 1904 a seventh edition appeared marking the centenary of the establishing of the British and Foreign Bible Society. In the latter, Charles explained to readers:

---

5 Thomas Jones wrote three booklets exposing the errors of Arminian theology in 1806, 1807 and 1808. Jones informed readers that the booklets had been approved by the Association as well as by Charles and John Evans of Bala.

6 Only twelve issues were published from March 1809 to November 1813.

7 In Welsh (1801) and English (1805).

The work contains the meaning of untranslated Scripture words;
short exposition of all the chief subjects of the religion of Christ;
explanations of many Scripture passages; an account of the
fulfilment of prophecies; the histories of the various nations,
kingdoms and cities; their positions and surroundings mentioned
in the Scriptures. It gives the positions and heights of mountains;
the cycles of the hosts of the heavens, and their dimensions, Jewish
sacrifices, feasts and ceremonies; together with their references and
meaning as types of spiritual and evangelical things.[8]

Not only so, but Charles also included general information concerning
other countries regarding their religions, customs and languages
which would have been fascinating for readers but also useful for
those supporting overseas mission. What added to the value of
this work was his expert knowledge of the biblical text alongside
his grasp of historical theology and familiarity with Reformed
continental theologians like Turretin (1623–1687), Cocceius (1603–
1669) and Witsius (1636–1669). Charles read most of their writings
in the original Latin. His primary aim, however, in this *Dictionary* was
to teach the Bible, for which he was well qualified with his excellent
grasp of biblical languages as well as Latin, and his familiarity with
the French, Dutch and German languages. Between 1804 and 1811
while writing the *Dictionary*, Charles was engaged on the biblical
text, editing versions before printing for the Bible Society and SPCK,
so his explanation of Bible words in his *Dictionary* was well-informed.
This work remains a treasure, but it was devoured avidly by believers
throughout Wales for many decades with its exposition of biblical
terms, doctrines and the Christian life. Professor E. Wyn James claims
that 'Thomas Charles' Geiriadur Ysgrythurol is one of the books that

---

8   DEJ, 11, 474.

most influenced the Welsh mind in the nineteenth century.'[9]

Press

Providence again! The growth of his schools coupled with the increase in literacy and the growing numbers of societies and converts made literature an urgent requirement. At first Charles majored on providing spelling books for his pupils, then a catechism in 1789, but there were difficulties printing these and other books. Places as far away as Trefecca, near Brecon in mid-Wales and Chester were used, but the distance created problems involving delays in obtaining early drafts for correction, then receiving printed copies. The printers lacked Charles' sense of urgency and were eager to obtain payment before copies were sold. Visiting Chester, Charles shared with friends his idea of establishing a press at Bala. They referred him to a young man, Robert Saunderson, a former apprentice with the Chester printer but then working in Liverpool. Charles contacted him and he agreed to move to Bala and manage the Bala press which he did successfully for years making Bala a major centre for printing in Wales. When, therefore, it came to writing the final version of his Catechism he had developed since 1789, the Bala press handled it efficiently.

Hyfforddwr (Instructor)

The Catechism is known in Welsh as the *Hyfforddwr* (*Instructor*)[10] and as many as 17,000 copies were first printed. There was a huge demand so that eighty editions were published during the nineteenth century. It was a bestseller! This has been compared favourably with the Westminster Assembly's *Shorter Catechism* with which Charles was

---

9 'David Charles (1762–1834), Caerfyrddin: Diwinydd, Pregethwr, Emynedd', JHS, 36 (2012), p. 35.

10 The full title was *Hyfforddwr yn Egwyddorion y Grefydd Gristnogol/ An Instructor in the Institutes of the Christian Religion.*

familiar. The title of Charles' Catechism is influenced by John Calvin's *Institutes* but the 271 brief questions and answers make it longer than the *Shorter Catechism* and it also includes more content. In Wales, children learnt the entire *Instructor* with proof-texts and recited them in Sunday schools/churches. The questions and answers here are direct, brief, often memorable and always supported by biblical references.[11] Take, for example, the opening question with its one-word answer so easy for children as well as adults to learn:

Q: *Who made you?*
A: *God:* Psalm 100:3.

However, some questions and answers were more demanding, yet so helpful to all:

Q: *What are the operations which are more especially attributed to them?* [Father, Son & Holy Spirit].
A: *Creation and Election to the Father; Redemption and Intercession to the Son; and sanctification to the Holy Ghost* [with verses like 1 Peter 1:2 used in support].

The 271 questions and answers end with a further question: *'How many commandments are there in the Law?'* The answer of course is *Ten.* But then they are required to repeat the Ten Commandments with three more questions concluding the Catechism: *'What do you chiefly learn by these commandments?'* The formal answer is: *'We learn two things: our duty towards God, and our duty towards our neighbour.'*

---

11 The *Hyfforddwr* began in 1789 as a pamphlet then it appeared in its final form in 1807. Charles wrote this catechism with the benefit of nearly twenty years of experience in teaching and catechising children and adults.

As expected, an explanation of these two aspects of our duty form the final two questions and answers.

Both his *Dictionary* and *Instructor* became indispensable tools for Christians, young and old, throughout Wales in teaching and safeguarding Bible doctrine for several generations.

Restricted

Towards the end of 1808 and early 1809, Charles' leg caused him considerable pain. Writing to Thomas Jones, Denbigh, he explained: 'I have not been a moment … free from pain… We have often expected its complete recovery and as often been disappointed. Now the severity of the weather affects it much. I have promised to be at Dolgelley the first Sunday in February to open the new chapel there; but my promises are not much to be depended upon in the state I am.'[12] Months of enforced rest enabled him to write, pray and reflect on urgent issues facing them like the ordination of Methodist preachers.

Ordination: 1811

Charles and other evangelical clergy in Wales were opposed to ordaining Methodist preachers as they wanted Methodists to function within, not in opposition to, the Established Church. How long could they keep the Methodist movement within the parish system? Evangelical clergy in Wales were few in number compared to their counterparts in England, while local clergy were often unconverted, unsympathetic, even opposed to the gospel. Sadly, the bishops disliked evangelical preaching and beliefs.

For seventy years, Methodists had remained within their parish churches, observing the ordinances of Baptism and the Lord's

12 DEJ, 111, 212-3

Supper there. Griffith Jones's influence on early Methodist leaders like Howell Harris and Daniel Rowland was strong. Even William Williams, Pantycelyn – converted through Howell Harris' preaching in Talgarth – embarked on an itinerant Methodist ministry only after the bishop refused to ordain him as a priest because of his Methodist sympathies. He then established and supported local Methodist fellowships yet Williams was not eager to ordain Methodist preachers. David Jones, Llangan, had many Methodists flocking to hear him preach and participate in parish communion but he opposed the ordination of Methodist preachers. Similarly, David Griffiths, Nevern, preached in Methodist societies but he, too, opposed the ordination of Methodist preachers so from 1811 confined himself to his parish ministry. Thomas Charles was not a lone voice therefore and he would not have received much practical support from England for his work if he had left Anglicanism earlier.

Change of mind

This issue was raised in 1756 but Howell Harris stopped discussion; again, in the 1807 Llangeitho Association debate on it was refused. In the 1808 Caernarfon Association, ordination was advocated then in the 1809 Association, Thomas Jones, Denbigh, argued in support of ordination. Charles missed both Associations so Jones reminded him of frustrations and issues of conscience for believers who refused for their children to be baptized in parish churches by 'un-awakened ministers'. He pointed to the marks of a church: The Word preached and the sacraments duly administered, as being essential. He himself proceeded to baptize children.

Eventually, Charles recognised the inevitability of ordaining Methodist preachers. One factor influencing him was the danger of division as well as the prevailing confusion concerning the issue.

During 1810, Charles acknowledged that in the Lord's providence the ordination of their preachers should proceed but reported, 'I never had so delicate a subject under my consideration as I had prejudices of an opposite nature to combat with. However, through the Lord's blessing upon my endeavours, I hope I have succeeded.' [13]

Having made the decision the careful planning of ordination services in the North and South Associations began with the choice of preachers to be ordained. Unanimous approval of names was required; in the North eight men were chosen including Thomas Jones, Denbigh, and John Elias, Llangefni, whereas thirteen men were ordained in the South Association, including Ebenezer Morris and Ebenezer Richards from Cardiganshire. Charles had the major task of preparing for the ordination services and was responsible for questioning the candidates concerning doctrine before requiring them to approve the Calvinistic form of church government and faithfully administer the ordinances. Charles recognised that a new denomination was being formed and the ordination, therefore, must be unlike the Anglican practice. No hands were laid on candidates, only the right hand of fellowship was extended, no bishop participated, no Bible was presented and the Lord's Supper was not observed in the service. Nor was it an Independent ordination for no local church was ordaining but rather the Connexion ordained men in recognition of their wider preaching ministries and local involvement.

Not all were happy with the ordination but Charles, despite his preference to remain within the Anglican fold, gave the newly ordained men his full support. One example occurred when Charles was preaching then serving the Lord's Supper in Llangeitho chapel.

---

13 DEJ, 111, 237-290.

He asked one of the newly ordained men, John Roberts, Llangwm, to assist him in distributing the bread and wine to a thousand people. Roberts had also preached there that day with Charles, but the elders objected to Roberts serving in the Lord's Supper so they stopped him from serving. Charles immediately ended the service with the congregation leaving in tears without receiving the ordinance. Charles then rebuked the elders and they were required in the Pembrokeshire Association to repent and promise not to repeat their action. Charles recognised the equal standing of clergy with those ordained by the Associations.

Progress

In spring 1812, Charles informed a London friend of considerable blessing in Wales. Charles felt himself 'kindled in a flame' in reporting the Lord's blessing. The situation, for example, in South Wales was 'most delightful' and reminiscent of Pentecost and in one society over 140 were accepted within eight weeks. 'All the young people in a *large* district' were affected spiritually while the Associations at Aberystwyth and Haverfordwest 'were very pleasing and profitable', with about 20,000 attending the former one. Charles had not seen anything like this 'for years past. Preaching was as easy as opening the lips... I shall never forget it!' This encouraged Charles as it was the fruit of his labours in Sunday schools. 'The Lord has done great things for us' with more being done 'in a few weeks ... than was done before in many years of painful labour'.[14]

Encouragement was needed. Years of intense labour, travel, opposition and illness with increasing pressures in leading the Methodist movement before the anguish of agreeing to the ordination of Methodist preachers had all taken their toll on Charles.

14 DEJ, 111, 419-20.

Such gospel progress was a further seal on the work and a major encouragement in Charles' closing years.

12 Charles' Influence in Ireland and Scotland

We need to retrace our steps a little at this point in order to illustrate Charles' concern and involvement in the development of Christian work in Ireland and Scotland. Charles felt tired, so in God's providence the cold weather in February and March 1807 confined him to his home briefly. Charles was nevertheless greatly encouraged. His circulating schools and Sunday schools were prospering with hundreds of children having been catechised in previous weeks, Bible passages memorised and thousands of people listening to him preaching God's Word. 'I never saw the fields so universally ripe for harvest' he wrote.[1] The growth of the work in Wales made him question whether he could visit London as he normally did to attend the annual meetings of societies he was involved in. The reason was clear: 'the urgency of the work is so great' in Wales.

Ireland

There was also the prospect of his forthcoming visit to Ireland in early July that year, a trip he wanted to make because the spiritual,

1   DEJ, 111, 155

127

educational and moral needs of children and adults there had concerned him for some time. Earlier in 1806, the Hibernian Society[2] had suggested to Charles that he should visit Ireland to see their situation and encourage them.

There was also ongoing discussion within the committee of the British & Foreign Bible Society in London as to whether or not they should print Bibles and New Testaments in the Irish language. The subject was controversial, arousing strong feelings of support but also opposition. One opponent of publishing Bibles in the Irish tongue was an Irish clergyman who explained that the 'common people' could not read the Irish text and those who were taught to read were taught in the English language. Furthermore, there were differences between grammatical Irish and the Irish spoken daily by the people. The clergyman claimed to have considerable support for his position.

The clergyman's letter was eventually forwarded to Charles for his advice. Charles' response was detailed. He had heard that 'many hundreds of thousands of the Irish speak their native language, and do not understand English.' In fact, many more spoke Irish in Ireland than those who spoke Welsh in the Principality. All teaching therefore ought to be in their native language and they should be taught to read Irish, particularly with 'a good translation of the Bible' in Irish.

2 This was established in Dublin in 1764 in a deep concern for the many poor and destitute children of Irish soldiers who had left for duties overseas or who died in active service. A school was opened in 1765 for twenty children but the number of orphaned children increased. Funds were raised largely by Protestant communities in Cork and Dublin. The school curriculum included spelling, reading, writing, arithmetic and the learning of the Protestant catechism with a chaplain giving instruction in the Bible. They also learned a trade like tailoring, needlework, shoemaking and farming.

The London Hibernian Society for establishing Schools and Circulating the Scriptures in Ireland was established in 1806 on the initiative of two Dublin Anglicans. By 1823 it had 61,387 day pupils in its schools.

In addition, Charles recommended that they adopt the model of 'circulating Charity Schools' he had in Wales. Towards the end of his letter, Charles opens his heart: 'I feel much interested in behalf of the poor neglected Irish: had I understood their language, I should have gone over years ago, to see what could be done for their improvement and instruction.'[3]

Charles' visit to Ireland, therefore, in July 1807 was of immense importance to him but also to the Bible Society, as well as those in Ireland burdened to educate and teach their people the Protestant faith. The continuing uncertainty of the Bible Society regarding the printing of Irish Bibles only added to the urgency of his visit. Charles rode on horseback to Holyhead from Bala and joined up with three men from London who were accompanying him to Ireland. Among the three men was David Bogue (1750–1825), pastor of an independent church in Gosport, Hampshire, who was an ideal person to accompany Charles. They were both among the co-founders of the British and Foreign Bible Society in London and Bogue was passionate about mission. Born in Berwickshire and educated in Edinburgh University, Bogue had received the first three students to train for missionary work before his academy came under the care of the London Missionary Society in 1800. Yale University awarded him the honorary degree of doctor of divinity in 1815 for his contribution to theology and mission.

Charles and his companions sailed for Dublin on Friday 24 July with Charles and Bogue preaching in different churches while there. Charles observed with sadness the bitter divisions amongst Protestant Christians but by contrast the warmth of the welcome from ordinary Irish language speakers who felt an affinity with the

3 DEJ, 111, 158-9

visitor due to him being a Welsh language speaker. Comparing some Irish and Welsh words, Charles recognised he could soon learn the Irish language but lamented there were no textbooks available to enable him to do so.

Following his visit, Charles' detailed report to the committee of the Bible Society included the recommendation to proceed with the publishing of New Testaments in the Irish language, but with the hope that others would commit themselves to teaching the Irish-speaking people to read the Scripture in their language. His recommendation was accepted with the result that Irish New Testaments were printed and distributed in 1811. In the meantime, Charles was pleased that the Hibernian Society Report (1809) revealed that its Committee had 'at present under consideration a plan for establishing circulating schools in Ireland similar to those established in Wales, which have been remarkably successful in laying a foundation for the extensive Sunday schools in that principality. They have lately received a very important communication from the Rev. Mr Charles, upon the subject.[4] Charles would have been thrilled to hear of the 1812 Report of the Hibernian Society which reported that 'six young men had been placed under the supervision of a godly clergyman in the south of Ireland who were forming and conducting Circulating Schools in various parts, on a plan similar to that which has been found so extensively beneficial in North Wales … their success has exceeded expectation.'[5]

---

4   DEJ, 111, 351-2.
5   DEJ, 111, 353.

Scotland

The *Evangelical Magazine*[6] was launched in London in 1793 by two brothers from Wales, Evan and David Williams, as a monthly magazine aimed mostly at a readership of Christians embracing Calvinistic theology with its emphasis on the sovereignty of God in creation, providence and salvation. Evangelical dissenting pastors as well as evangelical Anglican clergy and laity supported the magazine. An Anglican vicar, John Eyre (1754–1803), edited the magazine until 1802. Charles' letters to the *Evangelical Magazine* appeared in 1808[7] and 1809 in which he described the success of his circulating schools and Sunday schools in Wales. Two brothers,[8] John Brown (1754–1832) of Whitburn and Ebenezer Brown (1758–1836) of Inverkeithing, who were both influential ministers of the gospel in Scotland were impressed by what Charles had written in the *Evangelical Magazine*. They had been concerned for some time about the spiritual and educational needs of people, young and old in the Scottish Highlands with John having encouraged itinerant preaching among the English language speakers, but gradually both brothers also became concerned for Gaelic speakers in the area.

By 1807–1808, the Brown brothers became troubled over the spiritual needs of Highlanders who moved to the fertile areas in the south of Scotland for the autumn period either to help in harvesting crops or as cattle-drovers. The brothers obtained tracts and Scripture portions from the Bible Society for the purpose of giving them freely to these workers along with a copy of their father's Catechism. These

---

6 The *Christian Observer* was launched in 1802 catering for evangelical Anglicans with the result that Congregationalists had an increasing role in continuing the *Evangelical Magazine* with its strong missionary interest.

7 1808, Supplement (571-2) and April 1809 (173-5) and May 1809 (217-8).

8 The sons of the well-known Rev. John Brown (1722–1787) of Haddington.

were well received. Charles' correspondence in the *Evangelical Magazine* at that time describing the success of his work in Wales impressed many readers in different church denominations. John and Ebenezer Brown were encouraged through reading about Charles' work and Ebenezer lost no time in writing to Charles describing the desperate educational needs in the country and the prevailing ignorance concerning the Christian faith. The letter[9] was detailed but the brothers requested more information concerning the methods used in Wales in establishing circulating schools.

Charles shared this need with friends in London and in the Lord's providence, an Edinburgh Baptist pastor, Christopher Anderson, visited London to learn more about the work of the Bible Society. It is uncertain whether he met Charles on that visit but on returning to Scotland, Anderson recommended the formation of an Auxiliary Bible Society to be based in Edinburgh. The burden of the Brown brothers was felt by Anderson who explained: 'My heart bleeds for the Highlands and the Islands of Scotland. We have the prospect of something being done for them soon.'[10] He wrote to Charles requesting more information about his schools. In response, Charles gave details about his work and shared how he had been in contact with the Rev. Ebenezer Brown concerning the same matters.

Replying to Anderson in January 1811, Charles[11] felt encouraged that in Scotland there was now the real possibility that the 290 schools managed by the Scottish SPCK could be supplemented by circulating schools similar to those in Wales. Charles' letter was detailed and practical, containing reflections on his work over twenty-three years. The beginnings were 'small, but the little brook

---

9 20 September 1809

10 Writing to Mr Fuller in November 1810

11 4 January 1811

became an overflowing river, which has spread widely over the whole country in Sunday schools…' Charles provided six persuasive reasons why young people should be taught in their native language, two reasons being that it helps the young to learn English afterwards 'much sooner' and it 'proves to them we are principally concerned about their souls, and … the vast importance of acquiring the knowledge of divine truths, in which the way of salvation, our duty to God and man, is revealed…' He added that children 'are candidates for another world, and that the things pertaining to their eternal felicity there are of infinitely greater importance to them, than the little concerns which belong to our short existence…'

Anderson valued Charles' letter 'with a most interesting account of all that has been done in Wales since 1731…' On the 11th January 1811, 'The Society for the Support of Gaelic Schools was formed with the only object of the society to teach the inhabitants to read the Holy Scriptures in their native language.'[12] In his response to the news, Charles congratulated Anderson and his friends on this success. He also wrote to the Rev. Ebenezer Brown: 'Little did I conceive, when I wrote to you respecting the state of the Highlanders, what the issue of our correspondence would be. I am extremely happy that the work is begun … but by the blessing of the Lord on the day of small things, we may confidently expect great things in the Lord's good time.'[13]

To encourage and guide the new Gaelic Society committee in Edinburgh, Charles sent a parcel of the Rev. Griffith Jones's *Welsh Piety*[14] which related the emergence and development of his

---

12 First Annual Report, 7-8.

13 DEJ, 111, 371

14 *Welsh Piety: or the useful charity of promoting the salvation of the poor. Being an account of the rise, method, and progress of the circulating schools.*

circulating schools in Wales in the eighteenth century. These schools, emphasised Charles, 'were attended with the greatest blessing'. For Anderson especially, the *Welsh Piety* accounts were invaluable and the Report of the first annual meeting of the Gaelic Society contained many quotations from it.

Charles' influence, therefore, was not confined to Wales for Ireland, Scotland and England benefited greatly from his preaching, vision and support. His vision was international as he anticipated worldwide blessing as the gospel of Christ was preached in different countries.

Our need in the twenty-first century is great, but the God of Thomas Charles is also our God and is able in our generation to revive His church in unimaginable ways for His glory. A huge and contemporary challenge for us!

13 Family Life: Closing Years

May 1810 was an important milestone because Sally retired from the shop and their son, Thomas Rice, who had partnered Sally for two years in the business, now assumed full responsibility. Early in 1810 she suffered a stroke and in March, Charles revealed, 'I am hardly a moment from her through the whole of the day.' Late in 1811 Sally suffered a second stroke while in a fellowship meeting. Charles reported to their close friend Lydia Foulkes in Machynlleth that she was 'rather worse … and been very low'. A clear mind, however, enabled her later to meditate on the Word, using Caryl's detailed commentary on Job. The Lord was precious to her though 'seldom … without her doubts and anxious fears'. Charles was 'very loath' to leave her, to preach away from home, but when he did so Lydia Foulkes' daughter Mary stayed with Sally for a week or two. One such occasion was in April 1812 when Charles toured areas in South Wales. He was encouraged because 'the Schools appeared prosperous in most parts' and he saw this as 'an ample reward for all my labours these twenty-six years'. The Lord was working powerfully. By the autumn of 1812, Sally's health had improved, though 'still an invalid' and he felt he could 'venture' to travel, though he trembled thinking about it.

Alongside caring for his wife, therefore, Charles continued a reduced schedule of itinerant preaching, overseeing the schools, supporting associations and even visiting London. One London visit was for a month in April/May 1813 where he agreed to edit and proofread a new edition of the Welsh Bible, published a year later. When at home he was busy on such projects, including writing *Rules for Establishing and Organising the Sunday Schools* and compiling a Welsh Bible concordance.

Health issues at home increased. While on a preaching tour of North Wales early in 1813, he received news that his eldest son, Thomas Rice, was 'very dangerously ill' at home. He recovered slowly but sadly neither he nor his younger brother, David Jones Charles,[1] were believers. By the autumn, Charles himself began to suffer considerable weakness which doctors attributed to 'over-exertion of body and mind'. He explains: 'I have been for these two months past and more in a state of great bodily debility... I had frequent pains and was confined to the house, and I was frequently on the bed. I was not fit for anything that required exertion either of body or mind.'[2] He was advised to rest, and improved with his care of Sally continuing, despite regular bouts of weakness.

Faith

Charles felt stronger by March 1814 while Sally remained 'feeble and entirely confined to the house'. Mary and Sarah Foulkes in turn were his main support in caring for Sally. His personal faith shone at this time of weakness and caring: 'My poor invalid wife continues feeble

---

1 The brothers were aged 29 and 19 respectively.

2 DEJ, 111, 487

and is entirely confined to the house, though not to bed. She is too feeble to walk hardly any... All these little concerns of health are in the Lord's hands, and it cannot be better. It is well when we are able to acquiesce in his disposal of us in all things. He has a right to dispose of us and he will do us no injury in the end.'[3]

Influenced by John Newton's example,[4] Charles had engaged in extensive letter writing over the years, endeavouring to counsel people in different circumstances. One of his many helpful letters was written on the subject of faith in September 1813 when a friend wanted to understand the nature of faith. Charles replied that months previously he gave his young people an exercise to discover all the names given to faith in the Bible. They worked diligently, discovering 'seventy-one names given to this grace in the Bible'. After learning 'all the references, they repeated them twice in our chapel'. Their references to faith included: 'believing Christ ... coming to Christ ... living upon him ... casting all our cares upon him ... trusting in him ... committing our way to the Lord ... resting in the Lord ... taking hold of his strength ... believing the Word ... looking to Christ...' Charles admitted he 'received more light upon this important subject than from all the authors I have ever read; and the effect still continues sweetly on my mind.'

That faith was real for Charles as he trusted and committed himself, his family and the work to his Lord. Major encouragements continued. For example, the June 1814 Bala Association was attended by between fifteen to twenty thousand people who would have listened to fourteen 'edifying and powerful' messages. The absence of disorder and drunkenness coupled with 'the order and decorum

---

3 DEJ, 111, 514

4 In earlier years, Charles had helped John Newton prepare some of his letters for publication.

which prevailed among such a large concourse of people, was great and pleasing. Nothing but the hand of God could preserve so much order among so many corrupted sinners so long together. It was the Lord's doing and it is marvellous, surpassing marvellous in our eyes.' Reflecting on Psalm 23 verse 6, Charles added: '…goodness and mercy have followed me all my days; and I have continued, preserved by undeserved, powerful grace to see the wonders of his kingdom. Great additions have been made to our churches last year… The Bible Societies, the schools and every good work set on foot, succeed among us … May the kingdom come speedily, O Lord.' He was still very much aware that 'it pleases the good Lord at present to order his Providence towards us. To be thankful in all things is our duty and privilege… Thankful! Surely it behoves those to be so, who have by free grace been saved from hell – and saved in such a way, what a wonder!'[5]

Death

Preaching near Bala on Sunday 24 July 1814, Charles collapsed while riding his horse home and fell unconscious to the ground. He slowly recovered and doctors advised him to go with Sally to Barmouth for rest. Both enjoyed the sea air but Charles also preached there, reminding his wife that 'the fifteen years are nearly completed', a reference to Richard Owen's prayer for a fifteen-year extension to his ministry when he had been dangerously ill as a result of frostbite. As promised, on their way home they stayed in Machynlleth with the Foulkes family where he preached for the last time. The preaching exhausted Charles and he was relieved to arrive home. Their son David Rice recovered from a serious illness, but their valued maid-

5   DEJ, 111, 530-1

servant, Peggy, died, then Charles' health deteriorated rapidly over the following weeks.

Two days before he died, he repeated from Luke 2:29-30 the words of Simeon: 'Lord, now lettest thou thy servant depart in peace, according to thy word: for mine eyes have seen thy salvation.'[6] In his last sermon, Charles had preached on Romans 8:18 (KJV): 'For I reckon, that the sufferings of this present time are not worthy to be compared with the glory which shall be revealed in us,' with people commenting afterwards that, 'he seemed like one ripe and ready to escape from the bodily sufferings which then harassed him, to enjoy the glory that shall be revealed to all the people of God.' He died and entered glory on the 5th October, 1814.

Crowds of people met in the open air in Bala for the funeral service with Charles' close colleague for decades, Thomas Jones, preaching from Hebrews 11:4. The crowds with tears sang hymns as they walked from town, skirting the lake to reach the parish church cemetery at Llanycil nearby where he was buried. A profound sense of loss was felt. The Calvinistic Methodist denomination had lost its much-loved leader. In his sermon, Thomas Jones had said: 'Wales has cause to weep for him – for this loss; and a great loss it is … a loss to Britain…' We can also add 'a loss to the world'.

The impact of Charles' death on Sally was immense, affecting her memory and giving rise to considerable grief. Within three weeks, Sally died and was buried alongside her husband Charles in Llanycil church cemetery.

---

6   DEJ, 111, 545-6.

14 Personal Reflections

There are many relevant and challenging aspects arising from the life and work of Thomas Charles which merit serious consideration by Christians today. All I intend to do in this concluding chapter is to identify briefly a small number of these aspects which I have personally found humbling and exciting with the purpose of encouraging readers to ponder their contemporary relevance.

Becoming a Christian

Charles was privileged in many ways: having a loving family, learning Bible and Catechism in school, hearing good sermons, reading Christian books and having an elderly Christian who shared with him about the Lord Jesus. Several had prayed for Charles' conversion but the means of grace bore fruit when Charles was a student in Carmarthen, aged seventeen, when he was saved under the preaching of Daniel Rowland. He became more aware of his sin but was 'astonished' seeing Christ's love, power and sufficiency which brought him indescribable joy and peace.

His conversion is an encouragement. Sowing the Word faithfully and prayerfully in a family and church context is essential. Being under the Word preached is normally God's way of bringing individuals to faith in Christ, so preachers need to be prayed for regularly because God alone 'gives the increase' (1 Cor. 3:7). Are we sowing the Word faithfully? Do we depend on the Lord to draw sinners to Christ? Prayer is urgently needed.

Charles' conversion is also a warning. A child or adult can be well-taught in the Bible, hear gospel messages, enjoy Christian friends without becoming a real Christian. Charles acknowledged: 'I had some idea of gospel truths before floating in my head, but they never powerfully and with divine energy penetrated my heart until now.' The radical, inward work of the Holy Spirit in regeneration is essential (2 Cor. 5:17; John 3:3, 5 and 7). Are we looking prayerfully to God to do this divine work in the lives of unconverted relatives, friends and neighbours?

Bible

Charles' name is linked with the Bible. That is appropriate given the story of teenager Mary Jones walking alone, barefooted over mountains to Bala for a Bible, alongside Charles' role in meeting the increasing demand for Welsh language Bibles for his people and consequently in helping to establish the Bible Society in London.

To understand Charles' love of the Bible we must retrace our steps. His circulating schools and Sunday schools sought to enable poor, uneducated children and adults to read and understand the Bible. Copies of the Bible were scarce and too expensive to purchase. Charles therefore worked hard to have more copies of the Welsh Bible printed; he met with success but also frustrations. His success only added to his labours for his grasp of Hebrew and Greek made him the ideal person to edit and approve editions of the biblical text before printing. This was a labour of love for he treasured God's Word.

Months before he died, Charles wrote:

The Bible is a friend to all who love him, and can give them consolations, strong, divine and eternal… His advice is that of the highest wisdom and goodness, and may be safely relied on and followed… He will accompany you through death, as far as you need him…

The Bible was precious to him because it was of divine origin and inspired. This high regard for the Bible is expressed for example in *The Christian Instructor* [1], which he wrote:

Question 214: *'What are the ordinances and means of grace, which Christ appointed in His church?'*

He referred to:

a) *'the hearing of God's Word; and the searching of the Scriptures…*
b) *diligent prayer... and*
c) *the reverent and faithful use of the sacraments.'*

Question 221 asks: *'What is the Word of God?'* He answered: *'The Holy Scriptures of the Old and New Testaments: 2 Tim. 3:16'.*

Question 222 asks: What is *'understood by all the Scriptures being holy'.* Three answers are provided:

a) *'The holy God is the author of all the Scripture: 2 Peter 1:21*
b) *All the Scripture is holy in its nature; the commandments, the doctrine and the promises are all holy: Ps. 19:8-9*
c) *It is through the word that God sanctifies unholy sinners: John 17:17'.*

---

1 Chapter xii.

Question 223 poses a more practical question: *'Why ought we to hear the word?'* This question and answer require emphasis today:

a) 'Because it is God's word, and no man can reverence God without reverencing His word: 1 Thess. 2:13
b) Because 'faith comes by hearing, and hearing by the word of God': Rom. 10:17
c) Because preaching of the word is a divine ordinance: Matt. 28:19
d) Because we are instructed by the word in the things which pertain to our salvation: Rom. 15:4, John 5:39, 2 Tim. 3:15'.

Charles would rejoice to witness the availability and distribution of Bibles today in many languages but he also wanted people to read the Bible themselves, and become familiar with its message and Author. Do we neglect the Bible? To love God means also loving His Word – that is Charles' message to us today.

Providence

Frequently Charles and Sally had each referred to providence! In the *Christian Instructor*, affirming God as Creator and God's glory as the purpose of creation, **Question 23** asks: *'Does God uphold and govern the world which he created?'* The emphatic answer is: *'he does; he upholds and rules over all things: Ps. 103:19, Col. 1:17'*. That is what providence means.

Charles believed providence gave him as a teenager the friendship and prayers of Rees Hugh. Again, 'providence very unexpectedly and very wonderfully opened' the door to study in Oxford. The network of friends he made in Oxford and wider afield like John Newton was strategic for his future work. God planned those friendships. 'Puzzled' at times as to what was happening in his life yet he had a 'secret trust' in the Lord. Recognising the door closing on a Worcester curacy, he wrote: 'The Angel of the Lord with his sword drawn in his hand, obstructs my way to Worcester. The will of the Lord be done… I hope to follow the fiery cloudy pillar wherever it may lead…' That same conviction governed his courtship and then married life with Sally. For months before he and his wife died, they recognised that their circumstances were lovingly ordered by the sovereign will of God.

In our contemporary secular society, this doctrine of providence is neglected and the term infrequently used. The world does not revolve around oneself or any personal whims or pleasures we have but around our glorious, triune God. He is in absolute control everywhere and all the time.

Courtship and marriage

We have seen that Charles heard about Sally from Christians while studying in Carmarthen and he liked what he heard about her Christian character. They lived nearly two hundred miles apart and travel was difficult, so there was no possibility of meeting Sally. It was several years before they met (1778). He was impressed by her. A year then elapsed before he wrote to her and made clear there was no one else he wanted to spend his life with and he was not motivated by her money. Correspondence continued but it was another two years before he was able to visit her again.

From their correspondence one detects how, despite doubts about the relationship and a resolute unwillingness to leave Bala, she responded to Charles' caring, pastoral approach to her lack of assurance and fears. She shared more increasingly and both were encouraged in praying for one another. Charles emphasised that love was neither grounded in physical attraction nor motivated by ulterior motives but rather in settled convictions and care for one another. The Lord, too, must be at the centre of the relationship. In their marriage, Sally cared for the shop and family, and her income from the shop supported the family and Charles in his ministry. Both accepted that Charles needed to be away from home for days or weeks at a time for the sake of the gospel. Prayer and love characterised their home, with Charles caring for his wife faithfully until they were parted by death.

Their courtship and marriage pose challenges for Christians today. Infidelity, pornography, a rising divorce rate with its devastating impact on the family unit, domestic abuse, the denial by increasing numbers of people of the creation ordinance of marriage, compel us to ask questions afresh as to what it means to fall in love with a person of the other sex and commit oneself to lifelong marriage. Are we as churches providing adequate biblical guidance in these areas? Are married couples and their families seeking first God's kingdom and righteousness (Matt. 6:33)? Reflecting on the story of Thomas Charles can be both helpful and extremely challenging in this respect. Here was a man who lived a consistent Christian life and nowhere was it more obvious than in his marriage and family. He loved and pastored his dear wife well.

Word and Spirit

Here is a key relationship for Christians. Nothing is more important than what God says in His Word. God's objective Truth is supreme and should govern our thinking and lives. These were convictions Charles held to firmly. Nevertheless, Charles was also convinced from Scripture that without the Holy Spirit, the Word is lifeless. The Holy Spirit alone opens blind eyes and changes sinners inwardly in the miracle of regeneration; the Spirit also quickens and strengthens believers through the Word. And as Charles was essentially a preacher[2] eager to proclaim the Bible's central message concerning God's amazing love and purpose in Christ, he felt utterly dependent on the Lord. Prayer, for Charles, was not an option but a necessity. Only the Lord could prosper the Word preached.

One more aspect of this relationship is relevant. Charles was deeply moved in the Word in different situations. During his illness, for example, in 1800 the Lord gave him 'such glorious views of HIMSELF as produced a comfortable, calm frame of mind and *joyful* resignation to his will'. He continued: 'I never had such views before … in the same degree of clearness and continuance of his sovereignty, and justice … goodness and tenderness… It was an amazing sight, by faith, of a crucified Saviour… I could not help loving him, and having confidence in him, and rejoicing with joy unspeakable and full of glory…'

For Charles, Bible truths and theology must lead to a closer, intimate fellowship with Christ and therefore he depended on the Holy Spirit to make this experiential aspect of union with Christ very real through the Word. How real is the Lord to us as Christians? Do we enjoy the Lord in the Word and in prayer? To put it bluntly, are we taking seriously the inseparable but dynamic relationship between the Word and the Holy Spirit?

2 In February 1814, the year of his death, he wrote to a friend about preaching. He acknowledged that not all men could preach extempore but added: 'I could never read my sermons, nor make use of skeletons, without being much embarrassed.' The content of preaching should be 'thoroughly evangelical… with plainness and zeal'. People must understand the message but, 'Be earnest about the salvation of your hearers… If other writers' sermons are better than what Charles and his contemporaries can compose, use them for the present; but do not leave off composing. Study the Bible, and compose something in divinity every day of your life.' DEJ, 111, 512.

Revival

In September 1784 Charles asked Sally to pray: 'I long to see past times of the outpouring of the Spirit returning again.' He had seen the impact of the 1762 and 1778–1782 revivals on North Wales but longed to witness the Lord working again in extraordinary power. His burden was for many people to be saved and the church to enjoy and glorify the Lord. The majority of people were unsaved and churches needed stirring again. His prayer was answered abundantly.

Referring to revival in Bala (1791), he explained: 'I would not have been without seeing what I now see in the land – no, not for the world.' He shared: 'It is an easy and delightful work to preach the glorious gospel … with irresistible energy, accompanying every truth delivered…'

Notice what Charles says. Preaching the gospel was suddenly made extraordinarily powerful and effective with large numbers of people saved in a brief time. The ongoing work of the Holy Spirit in believers is essential but there are degrees of His working and occasions decided by the Lord when He works in exceptional power to save many people, transform a community while also enlivening churches in overwhelming believers with a sight of God's amazing love in Christ. That is revival.

In Charles' *Instructor*, the Spirit's 'ordinary' or normal working is referred to in chapters vii-ix. 'Through the Word and the ordinances of the Gospel', the Holy Spirit brings sinners to Christ, 'sanctifies, seals, strengthens and instructs them continually.' That is true of every Christian.

However, promises in the Word like John 16:7, Matthew 7:7 and Luke 11:13 encourage us to seek the Lord for further degrees and manifestations of the Holy Spirit's power. The same Holy Spirit working in believers also erupts on occasions in extraordinary power so that vast multitudes of people, Jews and Gentiles, can be saved within a brief period of time. Relying on the divine promises in the Word, assured of the Lord's covenant faithfulness and omnipotence, Charles and his contemporaries sought the Lord with confidence to pour His Holy Spirit upon the church. Time and time again the Lord answered their prayers.

Conclusion

Thomas Charles 'was the Lord's gift not only to the whole of Wales, and not only to the whole of Great Britain but also to other countries and nations afar off'.[3]

The life and work of Thomas Charles present major encouragements as well as challenges for churches and Christians worldwide in the twenty-first century. But please remember his words that 'there are no difficulties with God'!

---

3 General Assembly 'History of the Calvinistic Methodists', revised edition 1990.

Also available from Christian Focus Publications…

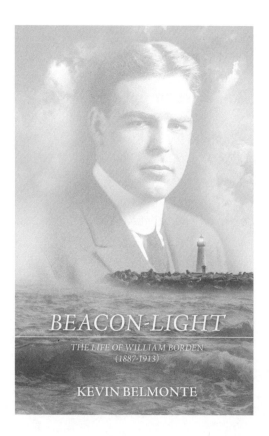

BEACON-LIGHT

THE LIFE OF WILLIAM BORDEN
(1887-1913)

KEVIN BELMONTE

Beacon–Light

The Life of William Borden (1887–1913)

Kevin Belmonte

The fascinating story of a young millionaire whose short life was lived in the service of his Lord.

Although William Borden was taken from this world at the young age of 25, the years he lived were full of dedication to serve. Kevin Belmonte draws on letters, quotations and images to paint a unique picture of William's life of commitment to God, delving into the ways 'vital truth,' as William called it, was the star he reckoned by. In the telling of the life story of William Borden, there is much to learn about living a life of devotion to God. The desire to live for Christ guided and shaped William's life, from his school days, right up until his death.

In the tradition of Chariots of Fire *and Eric Liddell, William Borden's story reveals the hand of God at work in a remarkable way…Kevin Belmonte has brought to life another story from history that we desperately need today.*

Chris Fabry
Moody Radio, host of 'Chris Fabry Live'

… a vivid, cinematic telling of William Borden's life, his deep compassion, and the large circle of his friendships. Faith illumined his brief but vibrant life. In the ivy halls of college, and beyond, he knew the True North of belief.

Kelly Monroe Kullberg
Editor and co–author of *Finding God at Harvard,*
founder of The Veritas Forum

978-1-5271-0719-9

BY JOHN W. KEDDIE

RUNNING
THE RACE

ERIC LIDDELL
OLYMPIC CHAMPION & MISSIONARY

Running the Race

Eric Liddell – Olympic Champion and Missionary

John W. Keddie

The name Eric Liddell is a familiar one to many, having gained much fame through the film *Chariots of Fire*. A Christian athlete and missionary, his passion for his Saviour could be seen throughout his life. From university days to internment at Weihsien POW Camp, John Keddie's biography brings together a specialist understanding of both Liddell's faith and sporting achievements to provide an engaging account of this normal man's extraordinary life.

Former athlete and churchman John Keddie brings both sporting expertise and spiritual insight to this lucid and meticulous biography of the great Eric Liddell.

Sally Magnusson
Broadcaster (Reporting Scotland, Songs of Praise) & author of several books, including *The Flying Scotsman: The Eric Liddell Story*

Like many, I shall never forget the impact of my first viewing of Chariots of Fire, *where a portion of the life–story of the Scottish Christian sportsman Eric Liddell was told. It was deeply inspiring and proved to be the foundation of an ongoing interest in Liddell's life. So I am thrilled to recommend this fresh biographical study of Liddell by John Keddie: perfect to inspire a new generation, it is powerfully written and beautifully illustrated. A joy to read.*

Michael A. G. Haykin
Professor of Church History and Biblical Spirituality,
The Southern Baptist Theological Seminary, Louisville, Kentucky

978-1-5271-0531-7

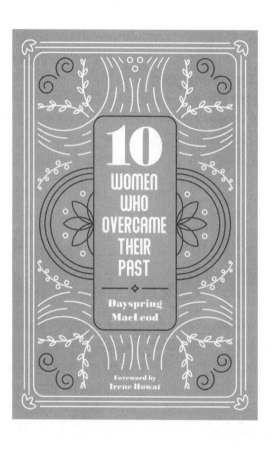

10
WOMEN WHO OVERCAME THEIR PAST

Dayspring
MacLeod

Foreword by
Irene Howat

10 Women Who Overcame Their Past

Dayspring MacLeod

This book contains the stories of ten women whose circumstances and choices led them to a place that seemed far removed from the fruitful, joy-filled life we are called to live in Christ. But each of their stories is a testament to the work God does through His imperfect children. Their stories will encourage and inspire, and remind you that you are not alone in your struggles.

You'll want to read 10 Women Who Overcame Their Past *and rejoice in our redeeming, victorious Lord and Savior, whose yoke is easy and whose burden is light.*

Kristen Wetherall
Author of *Humble Moms, Fight Your Fears* and co-author of
Hope When It Hurts

Through these stories, we see women who overcame, but not in their own power and strength; rather, through the redemptive work of Christ on their behalf. In reading 10 Women, *you'll meet sisters in Christ whose lives and testimony both encourage and equip you to turn to Christ, the author and perfecter of your faith.*

Christina Fox
Counselor, retreat speaker and author

978-1-5271-0787-8

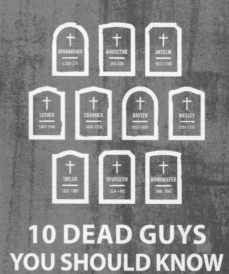

10 DEAD GUYS
YOU SHOULD KNOW

—

STANDING ON THE SHOULDERS OF GIANTS

EDITED BY IAN J. MADDOCK

10 Dead Guys You Should Know
Standing on the Shoulders of Giants
Ed. Ian J. Maddock

This collection of ten short biographies will introduce you to Christians from a variety of places and times, who all boldly preached the gospel, despite the risk to personal reputations and safety. How short-sighted it would be not to glean insights from our ancestors, whether that entails learning how to walk in their steps – or else avoiding their missteps.

… the lives, thinking and impact of ten of the most important 'dead guys' have been brought to life. Famous names become interesting characters and big ideas are explained simply and clearly in a way that shows why they are still important today.

Clare Heath-Whyte
Speaker and author of several books, including *Everyone a Child Should Know* and *First Wives' Club*

Each snapshot combines a brief biographical presentation with important lessons for the church to learn about obedience, faith, holiness, perseverance, courage, and mission. If readers are not familiar with these ten towering figures from the past, this book will bring them alive for today!

Gregg R. Allison
Professor of Christian Theology,
The Southern Baptist Theological Seminary, Louisville, Kentucky

978-1-5271-0608-6

Christian Focus Publications

Our mission statement –

STAYING FAITHFUL
In dependence upon God we seek to impact the world through
literature faithful to His infallible Word, the Bible. Our aim is
to ensure that the Lord Jesus Christ is presented as the only hope
to obtain forgiveness of sin, live a useful life and look forward to
heaven with Him.

Our books are published in four imprints:

CHRISTIAN
FOCUS

Popular works including biographies,
commentaries, basic doctrine and
Christian living.

CHRISTIAN
HERITAGE

Books representing some of
the best material from the rich
heritage of the church.

MENTOR

Books written at a level suitable
for Bible College and seminary
students, pastors, and other serious
readers. The imprint includes
commentaries, doctrinal studies,
examination of current issues and
church history.

CF4•K

Children's books for quality Bible
teaching and for all age groups:
Sunday school curriculum, puzzle and
activity books; personal and family
devotional titles, biographies and
inspirational stories – because you are
never too young to know Jesus!

Christian Focus Publications Ltd,
Geanies House, Fearn, Ross-shire,
IV20 1TW, Scotland, United Kingdom.
www.christianfocus.com
blog.christianfocus.com